Rambles around Nottingham and Derby

Keith Taylor

Published by Sigma Leisure – an imprint of
Sigma Press, 1 South Oak Lane, Wilmslow, Cheshire SK9 6AR, England.

British Library Cataloguing in Publication Data
A CIP record for this book is available from the British Library.

ISBN: 1-85058-324-2

Typesetting and Design by: Sigma Press, Wilmslow, Cheshire.

Maps by: Morag Perrott

Text photographs: Keith Taylor

Printed by: Manchester Free Press
Unit E3, Longford Trading Estate, Thomas Street,
Stretford, Manchester M32 0JT. Telephone 061 864 4540

General Disclaimer

Whilst every effort has been made to ensure that the information given in this book is correct, neither the publisher nor the author accept any responsibility for any inaccuracy.

Preface

"And when did you start walking?" someone asked me recently; and for a second I was thrown while attempting a straightforward answer. The fact is I can barely recollect a time when I was not walking or exploring and delving into some aspect of the natural and local scene.

As a boy born in wartime, I was encouraged to walk everywhere within a radius of five or six miles and was fortunate in having parents who regarded a bus ride as a luxury.

Sunday was 'walking day'; especially for Dad and myself, sunshine or sleet regardless. In the summer we were joined by Mum throughout the evening and our route intentionally byepassed a low beamed pub.

School was one and a half miles from home and there was no bus. But I walked home for dinner and back again in the early afternoon, so that by the time I had absconded each evening into one of my dens, fashioned from an elder thicket on the derelict land at the top of the road, I had already walked six miles.

When I was eight or nine I answered to the lure of the canal towpath with its beckoning bends and dusks spent around kindling fires,with colliers who had been swimming or gypsies settling in for the night. And it was from these wanderers that I learned of the Hermit's Cave at Dale Abbey, the Hemlock Stone near Bramcote and Swansea Bridge hidden from the billowing chimneys of Stanton and Stavely.

To reach such places I walked, at least until I could persuade my by then widowed mother to buy me a bicycle. Thus I discovered the landscape; its people, industries and rural communities, that encircles two thriving Midland cities.

Though some industries have long ground to a halt, the building of the M1 Motorway has created a belt of sound and speed that interprets industrial and regional connection. Yet access roads, dual carriageways and road widening schemes have failed to decimate the charm of hidden villages, cattle grazed meadows and quiet waterways.

Even at night the winter bracken fronds highlighted by the tapering flares of car headlights create that essential sense of place and serve further to remind us that miles of footpath, towpath and bridleway invite furter exploration. So why not put this book and a couple of maps into your haversack and accept that intriguing invitation, for there is much to be seen and perhaps new friends to be made while you arerambling around Nottingham and Derby.

Keith Taylor

CONTENTS

THE WALKS

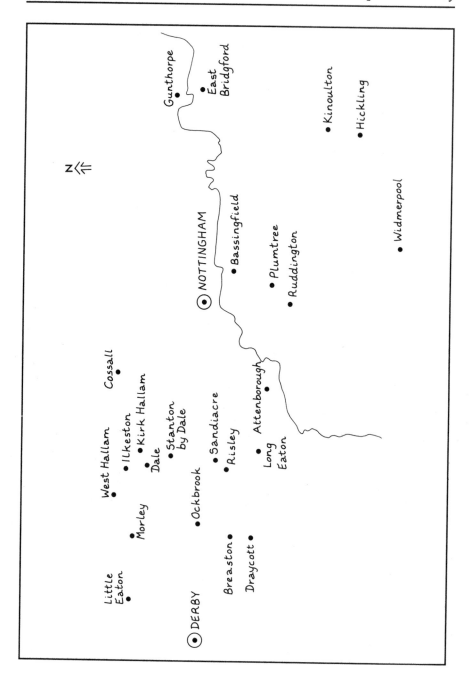

Walk This Way . . .

This book is intended for people who like myself and friends enjoy a regular ramble across varied and interesting tracts of countryside.

The walks I have chosen are based between and around the expanding cities of Nottingham and Derby. Whichever route the rambler decides to take, the pace of modern living may be represented by no more than the television aerials and the inevitable row of telegraph wires that we have learned readily to accept.

Out among the wildflower meadows connecting Kirk Hallam to Dale, you may meet only a couple walking their dog. At Widmerpool, south of the Trent, there could be a lone walker photographing the church. The paths are explored by relatively few; fewer in fact than

One of the many stiles and waymarks on the walks in this book

when I was a boy wandering the woods and cattle meadows some forty
years ago.

History

Nottinghamshire's history begins perhaps with early man's forays into
the forest and scrubland country north of the Trent. Two main forces for
survival would have attracted him there: food and shelter.

Relics from both the Neolithic and Bronze Age are widespread, and
boats hewn from tree trunks have been recovered from shallows
throughout the Trent Valley. These tell us that the river played an
important role as a hunters' route, alongside which some settlements
were established.

Spanning a direct route The Fosse Way (circa AD47) serves as a
memorial to the Roman occupation for along this stretch of road they
based four camps: Vernemetum (Willoughby), Margdurum (East Bridgford), Adpoten (East Stoke) and Rococolana (Brough).

The villas were self supporting and besides beans, rye, barley and wheat,
the occupants harvested surplus requirements of grain for export. Oats
were grown in the soils north of the county for the sole purpose of
feeding the cavalry horses, pack animals and oxen.

Using an early trackway extending from Derby and Little Chester to the
banks of the Trent, the Romans established a trade route along the river
– possibly to link with the River Witham near Lincoln. Food supplies,
ammunition and stone for building, were probably transported along
this route which the Romans called The Portway.

The Saxon Age was largely responsible for originating the place names
given in the following section. In the Domesday Survey of 1066
'Shirewood', the King's hunting ground, was referred to as a forest,
while an Earl's was known as 'a chase'. Thus we have Thorneywood
Chase situated near Carlton and Bakersfield.

Several pillars of stone in a roadside field at Old Clipstone near
Mansfield mark King John's hunting palace. Further east, the King

crossed the river at Kings Ford, which is close to the footpath-interlaced block of forestry and green open space, known today as Conjour Alders.

The Anglo Saxons were governed by a singular Royal Authority with the country divided into shires. Each lord or 'thane' was the recognised head or 'elder', who attended legal and administrative affairs at a shire court or moot. Most of the meetings revolved around land ownership and the forest laws, but deer populations were also discussed for the Conquers 'tall red deer' were regarded as 'beasts of the chase'.

James I, hunting in Sherwood Forest, recorded there having been 'two great stags the likes of which I have never before seen'. And Richard III was said to have been hunting deer at Bestwood, when he received word that Henry Tudor was waiting to do battle at Bosworth Field in Leicestershire.

West and south-west of Sherwood, settlements and small towns were separated by acres of forest scrubland, which in the south west was noticeably divided by low ridges and abutments of sandstone outcrop. Other than the scattered settlements, the nearest substantial trading town was Derby, then known as 'Deorby' which the Danes recorded as being 'the place of many deer, although the Romans who established a large camp there gave it the name of Derventio. This camp was situated near the eastern bank of the River Derwent and is today known as Little Chester.

By the time the Domesday Book was compiled, Derby had two thousand inhabitants, six churches and fourteen mills. Yet until the railway served its prominent purpose in both counties, there appears to have been no further expansion; at least in the materialistic sense.

Nottinghamshire's continuing heritage was commemorated in the bloody and bitter conflicts that followed when Charles I raised his Royal Standard a few yards from the gateway of Nottingham Castle on Monday 22 August 1642. Thus began the nine year English Civil War.

Newark Castle was besieged by Cromwell's Army and Nottingham Castle was fired by Colonel Hutchinson, its Royalist protector; a stream at East Stoke was renamed 'The Red Dyke' due to the bloody affray in which hundreds of men from both sides lost their lives. The water surface of the stream was said to have 'glistened red with the blood of the wounded and fallen'.

From the twelfth to the fifteenth centuries, families in both counties acquired wealth due to such merchandise as wool and woad. Others became millowners specialising in cotton and lace. Coal was another enterprise along with professional administrative positions like lawyers and bankers, so that eventually these families became recognised by the reigning monarch and occasionally knighthoods were given for recognition of various deeds and favours.

Living in a 'grand style' meant that large and imposing houses needed to be built in recognition of this wealth, and these were surrounded by parklands enclosed by pole fencing as a wall.

Thus today we have become familiar with such names and estates as the Willoughbys of Wollaton, Edges of Strelley, Chaworth-Musters of Annesley, Mundays of Shipley, Cokes of Melbourne and many more.

Landowners and farmworkers alike admirably adapted to The Enclosures Act to such an extent that the grounds of the average country house became partially landscaped. Coverts and plantations were established to provide gamebirds for the shooting gentry and to encourage foxes to breed, thus providing sport for the several well-known hunts.

With the coalfields extending and requiring transportation, came the Canal Age and Railway Era, both of which provided towpaths and disused routes for the walker to explore decades later.

In more recent times, most of the large country estates have been opened to the public and areas of derelict land and disused colliery tips been reclaimed for transformation into country parks and recreational areas. Acres of farmland and fewer belts of woodland remain to tempt the walker and occasional jogger along paths in sight of cooling towers, viaducts and aqueducts. Yet such paths always seem to provide some aspects of interest to those bound by ancestry and need to the great outdoors.

Place Names

Town and village place-names derive largely from the Anglo Saxon culture, which was predominant throughout the fifth and sixth centuries. The suffix 'ton or 'tun' indicates the whereabouts of a village or town, such as Elston, Leverton, Beeston and Ollerton.

According to the Domesday Book listings in 1086 there were eighty such settlements in Nottinghamshire and slightly fewer in Derbyshire, among them Breaston, Brampton, Burnaston, Carsington and Ilkeston.

Noticeably too were the 'ham' suffixes meaning homestead or enclosure and the Scandinavian ending of 'by' which is Danish for village.

On a more localised level, names ending in den, ley, hurst or field all refer to clearings in the forest and throughout the region these are well represented; each place with its own individual or 'parish' history. The Saxon Age is also commemorated by names or crossing points – 'fords' – along minor rivers like the Leen, Ryton, Medan and Maun.

The fords were usually the recognised crossing places of a chieftain, one of whom is thought to have been Bassa from which the name Basford (now pronounced Baseford) probably originated.

Huck was probably another Saxon leader whose home – or hall – The Hall of Huck was established in west Nottinghamshire, which in later centuries became known as Hucknall. Nearby Nuthall was regarded as 'the great place' (hall) – for storing crops of walnuts, hazelnuts and acorns.

The name Radford, however, suggests the whereabouts of the red (sandstone or clay) crossing place. And in Derbyshire, did Brail cross the tributary of the River Dane some six miles south east of Ashbourne? And Crom? If there was such a person, did he regularly ford one of those lovely streams? Finally, I should mention Borrwash; although today, we pronounce it as one word, the Anglo Saxons used the term 'borro-ash', which meant 'the tall ash tree beside the water'.

Farming

At the time of The Enclosures the average farm in this part of the country was growing barley, wheat, oats, beans, peas and clover and grazing seven or eight workhorses, nine cows and five or six calves, alongside sixty sheep.

In Derbyshire, because of the terrain, the sheep herds were increased by twenty or thirty head. A gentleman tenant farmer was paying the squire or landowner one hundred pounds per annum, while the latter's farm boasted finer stabling, cowhouses, milking sheds and larger granaries. Some farms had purpose-built ponds on which paddled a variety of ducks.

By the early eighteenth century wet or marshy tracks were drained by using tiles and the tasks of hedging and ditching were carried more regularly than they are today.

Between 1850-70 agriculture was a flourishing business, whether livestock or arable, because industry was also thriving alongside coal mining. Consequently there was an increase in the demand for food and agricultural journalists were not slow in referring to those twenty years as 'The Golden Age of English Farming'. When artificial fertilisers and machinery eased into the scene, several new and improved breeds of livestock were also introduced, with the English Longhorn cow being replaced by the Dairy Shorthorn, Guernsey and Ayrshire. Lincolnshire, Leicestershire and Suffolk sheep were persuaded to graze both the lowland fields and Derbyshire hills along with the native Blackface strain.

While Derbyshire today grazes large herds of cattle and flocks of sheep, the farms of Nottinghamshire are best described as mixed arable, for the soils are very varied, there being sandy, light and heavy clay soils throughout the region.

Most cereal crops, such as oats, barley and wheat are grown alongside potatoes, sugar beet and oilseed rape. The grassland is that which for long has been termed 'ley type' grass. This means that the grass is medium to short and besides providing grazing for livestock, it also produces silage and hay.

The farmsteads are a mixture of old and new buildings, often with a modern bungalow built alongside a now derelict traditional house. Many original outbuildings have been adapted to accept the modern agricultural theme and are used as dairies and storehouses etc. But still there are a few buildings made to look unsightly, because the farmer or landowner has chosen to use sheets of corrugated iron, rather than extend the business accounts to include the purchase of traditional bricks or pantiles. But fortunately such shoddiness is not widespread.

While walking the paths you will by-pass the tracks, trails and signs of such mammals as the fox, badger, hare, rabbit, grey squirrel and fallow deer. But whether you recognise them for what they are is a different matter.

The last red squirrels were recorded in 1955 and probably due to the effects of intensive farming and pesticides being washed down the drainage ditches and into the rivers, the last otters were sighted a decade later.

Mink, the wanton killers, are unfortunately widespread and increasing. In north Nottingham, muntjac and roe deer are infiltrating the forest glades, with the latter extending their range southwards from the woodlands of west Yorkshire and making a welcome return, for they had not been recorded in the county since the beginning of the Second World War.

Fallow deer abound in the woods and plantations around Stanley, Morley, Ockbrook and Annesley. An increase in numbers occurs throughout the Nottinghamshire 'Dukeries' where a small population of red deer can be found.

Vast populations of small mammals thrive in the banks and meadow grasses, a fact endorsed by the presence of predatory birds, the owls, hawks and falcons which breed in the woodlands and derelict farm and colliery buildings.

Garden and woodland bird species are well represented along with ground game and a rich variety of waterfowl; these latter birds cause the bird-watching groups to frequent the river valleys and gravel extraction areas throughout the autumn and winter months.

Leisure

Walkers often share the environment with birdwatchers, joggers, photographers, canal and narrowboat enthusiasts and in the season, anglers. And there is room for everyone.

Over the past five or six years there has been a sudden influx of golf courses, most of which have rights of way crossing them. Two stand out foremost as I write, perhaps because of the contrasts. The first that came to mind was the Cotgrave Place course with its landscaped lakes attracting wildfowl and the Erewash Valley course which connects Sandiacre to Stanton by Dale and is enhanced by acres of the medieval ridge and furrow system.

Horse riders also share the bridlepaths, particularly at the weekends. While they are as welcome as everyone else, one group has, in recent years, chosen to ignore the by-laws and churned up the towpath of the Grantham canal between Tollerton Lane and Bassingfield, making conditions difficult for the rambler during a damp winter. Since writing this paragraph, however, the towpath surface has been laid with a layer of chippings and hardcore which is an improvement.

Much of the land around and between the cities of Nottingham and Derby is contrasting countryside with dairy and arable farming thriving alongside private country estates, commercial blocks of Forestry Commission pine, and deciduous woodland owned by conservationist trusts or forming part of the local authority country park complex. Interwoven by disused railway cuttings, canals and several interesting minor rivers, the entire landmass is being continually encroached by industrial development, yet a rich variety of walks can provide both the family party and solitary outdoor enthusiast with a series of memorable outings. So here's to many clear mornings and mud-free gateways in the explorative days ahead.

Equipment and a few tips

When getting maps and books together for a ramble it is worth remembering that you'll probably have to carry the rucksack. It is best to travel light and although on most of these walks I have highlighted interesting pointers for the photographer and wildlife enthusiast, such items as a camera, binoculars or maps can be spread among the group.

Should you be fortunate in having two pairs of binoculars then obviously take the lightest, but preferably 8 x 40s or 10 x 50s. In my experience, however, you will see more wildlife species if you sit quietly with your outline broken up by overhanging foliage, than if you are walking the open fields and trackways.

Nor may you need binoculars if you are intent on watching a grass snake hunting for frogs in a ditch or disused canal. All you need do is stand quietly. If there is a chance of seeing birds, foxes and deer, then take them by all means.

Time

Allow plenty of time on all your rambles, as it is an unnecessary hassle to be marching against the clock on, for instance, a humid day in July or August.

Your Watch . . . and The Bus Driver's!

Just as no two people are alike, so are wrist-watches, and it is a safe bet that your watch will vary, perhaps by two or three minutes, from the one worn by your as yet unseen bus driver. Why not then play safe and put your watch forward ten minutes? That way you should arrive at the stop in good time.

Maps

In the introduction I have given details of the maps I have used for each particular walk. But I always recommend one of the Pathfinder Series of Great Britain (1:25,000). Maps can be borrowed from most local libraries, although it is always advisable to have a few neatly box-filed of your own. On one or two of the 'easier' walks, like Colwick Country Park, a map may not be needed as you are really following the bank routes around a chain of lakes.

Footwear

Walking boots are always advisable, particularly as most of the lanes and farm tracks are usually rutted with stones, intentionally laid in bygone times to provide purchase for the horses and farm carts. Boots also give that extra grip when you are climbing or descending steep banks. But trainers and wellingtons need never be frowned upon, providing you feel comfortable in them for a fair length of time.

Clothes

To thwart the vagaries of the British climate, always pack a cagoule during the summer. An anorak is often satisfactory in the spring and autumn and, for myself, I do like the deep pocketed Barbour thornproof-type jackets when winter walking and preferably with a detachable lining. A warm but lightweight sweater can also be packed during the colder months and knotted around the shoulders or waist if it proves uncomfortable. I also pack a hat, which in the summer helps fend off the midges and mosquitoes. Cotton socks with trousers tucked in are also ideal.

Miscellaneous

Be sure to take a suitable supply of food for a ramble, including snacks and drinks. A simple first-aid kit, including plasters for sore feet, is a sensible precaution.

Use the side pockets of your rucksack for storing the extra maps or a notebook and bus timetable, the latter preferably already turned to the applicable return journey. I doubt that you will need to take a flask as all the walks are within several miles of a welcoming hostelry.

Travel light and think beforehand. Then relax and enjoy the walks!

1. Around Little Eaton

The Route: Barley Close – EatonPark Wood – Peckwash Mills

Start: Barley Close off Alfreton Road, Little Eaton

How to Get There

By Car: A52 from Nottingham to Derby then the A61.

Parking: Bridge Inn Car Park, off Eaton Bank Road and begin walk from there.

By Bus: Trent 124-125-243 and 245, checking at either Nottingham or Derby.

Distance: 3.5 miles.

Duration: 2.25 hours with stops at viewpoints.

Maps: Pathfinder Series – Belper SK24/34

The Walk

This walk begins beside the signpost near the junction of Alfreton Road and Barley Close. What you are looking for is the steep uphill path and flight of stone steps rising between the houses.

Walk this steep path and cross the stile at the top. Turn left then walk to the stile beside the double signpost. When you are over this, turn right in the direction of Holbrook. The hedgerow should be to your right. On reaching the end of the field, climb the stile alongside the gate and cross to the corner of the field and those two gates.

Beside the left gate is a stile that you need to go over. The view overlooks Drum Hill and the Bottle Brook Valley while on the other side of the hedge is a gritstone wall, which reminds us of the Dark Peak country stretching away into the blue distanced north. Having walked

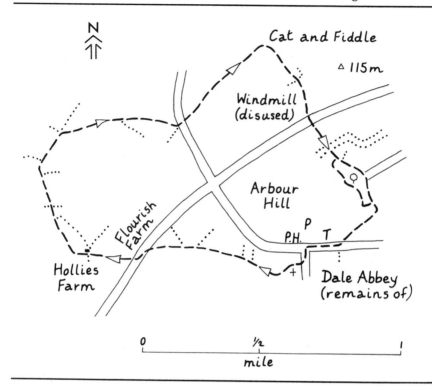

down the field to the stream, use the stepping stones and enjoy a stroll across the next meadow, particularly in June or July when you will no doubt recognize knapweed, ribwort plantain and meadow buttercup.

Climb the next stile and proceed along the right-hand hedgerow; while crossing this next field you may glimpse perhaps the lapwings and jackdaws which feed regularly in flocks.

When you reach the end of the field climb the stile well to the left of the gate. Then cross the wooden footbridge and make for the stile half way across the field. Climb this and you should next cross that narrow stream.

Ahead is Eaton Park Wood, so make towards its top left-hand corner. Continue through the gap in the hedge then turn right and head towards the field beside the wood. The wood is a good place to be listening to the songbirds in April or May. And you may glimpse a stoat, weasel or fox dependent of course upon the time of day.

Notice the high hedgerows bordering the narrow field; the fact that there is such a rich variety of trees and shrubs also informs us that they have been standing for many years and are beneficial to wildlife.

In the stone wall you will see a stile. Climb this and turn left along the bridleway. At the end of the wood take the stile into the field. You are now on an ancient route which the packhorse trains probably used when they journeyed from Wirksworth to Nottingham. There may have been between thirty and sixty horses in a column and each animal would have had a pannier either side of its saddle stocked with merchandise. This form of transportation was used until around the seventeenth century. While thinking of bygone times, follow this track for five fields and through the avenue of oaks probably planted to provide 'pannage' for a once-thriving population of pigs.

Views of the Trent, Dove and Quarndon valleys should be opening up around you; meanwhile you need to go through the corral to the small gate. The hedgerow here should be to your left.

Next follows a descent through the scrubland with a flight of steps at the foot of which you should turn left then right at the main road and continue down Eaton Bank. Before you reach Bridge Inn a footpath sign to your left directs you by the pub car park. Climb the stile then and cross the field towards the wood and that distinguishable chimney.

The church spire over to your right is that of St Alkmunds, Duffield. Although it dates from Saxon times, this place of worship has been much modified and little, if any, Saxon influence remains.

The next stile takes you into the wood with glimpses of the derelict Peckwash Mills, a paragraph about which is included in the adjacent notes.

Where the path ends, turn left onto Eaton Bank and then turn right. This eventually tapers into Duffield Road where you need the cobbled track sharply situated to your left.

Walk this then turn second right by the signpost and climb through the horse and sweet chestnut trees to the old quarry beside the stone bridge. This is a gritstone quarry and it was worked to produce stones for coping and for sinks and troughs. Whetstones for sharpening scythe blades were also extracted from such quarries as this.

The path leads to Vicarage Lane. Turn left and walk to Park Farm then proceed through the farmyard with the house on your right. You next need to climb the cross style in front of you then go across the field and back to the double signpost where you'll recognize the steps that, with care, will take you to your starting point.

The Peckwash Mills – Little Eaton

These gritstone mills were established in the late eighteenth century. The roof of the main building is slate; the chimney a landmark admired by visitors and locals alike. Throughout its working life the building has produced a variation of essential items, but by the nineteenth century was recognised as one of the largest paper manufacturing mills in this country.

Sadly, these mills have long fallen derelict, but there are people who, like me, believe that a working life could be restored, especially if they were used to house a local industrial museum or craft workshops.

2. Around Morley: The Roman Walk

The Route: Cloves Wood, Dabbs Hill Plantation – The Mound – Morley Smithy

Start: Off the A608 about half a mile south of the Rose and Crown Morley is a lay-by beside Cloves Wood. Park here.

How to Get There

By Car: From Derby, take the A608. From Nottingham, take the A52 to Chaddesden then turn right onto the A608 or the A609 through Ilkeston.

By Bus: Trent 123 – check at the Enquiries Office for times.

Distance: 5 miles

Duration: 2.5 – 3 hours

Maps: Pathfinder Series – Belper SK24/34

The Walk

At the layby climb the stile road and walk with Cloves Wood on your left, noticing the fox trails in the undergrowth. Where the wood ends, continue over three fields with electricity pylons on your right and look north-west towards Belper and the foothills of the Derbyshire Dales.

When you reach the house that may once have accommodated an estate steward and later a farm manager, climb the stile on the left and cross another field to the road.

Turn left and head for the junction then follow the road around to the right by-passing Cloves Hill Farm.

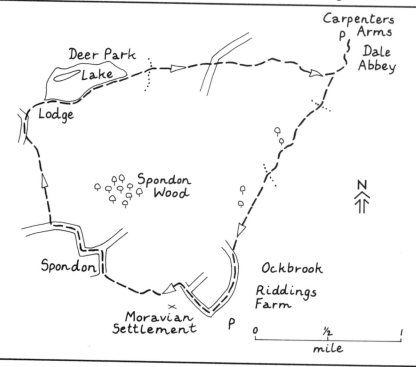

When you reach the signpost on the bend, turn left and over the stile and climb two more stiles while making for the gate directly ahead.

Morley, as you will already have noticed, is very much equestrian country and few are the fields hereabouts not grazed by horses and ponies.

Go through the gate and as you are crossing the next field make for the stile in the top right-hand corner. Climb the stile and again bear uphill to the field's right-hand corner, then continue up the hill and pass beneath the power lines to the next stile. Pause to take in the fact that the path crosses the Roman Road which was called Rykneld Street. This connected the Fosse Way at Bourton on the Water in the Cotswolds to Templeborough route, near Rotherham. An interesting route, where we are able in present times to tread the exact path used by the mobile workforces and Roman legions.

Ahead is Brackley Gate Farm. Walk towards it keeping that gritstone wall to your right then swing left and locate the stone stile which takes you onto the main road. This is known as Brackley Gate.

Make a right turn here, then walk with Honeywood Catteries on your left. Proceed along the green lane through Dobbs Hill Plantation which, being a largely coniferous wood, attracts cole-tits and Britain's smallest bird, the goldcrest, one or two pairs of which breed here.

Nuthatch and lesser and greater spotted woodpecker also feed and breed here, for such woods and plantations are included along the 'flight lines' of these insect feeding birds. After walking for half a mile or so, climb the stile to your left and enjoy a walk up through the wood and across the Breadsall Moor golf course following those marker posts to Morley Lane.

After the disused quarry to your left bear left and walk to Priory Cottages and the signpost opposite. Then climb the stile and walk with the stone wall on your right until you reach the next stile.

After climbing this keep the hedge and wall to your left and follow the narrow path through the grass and dog's mercury to Moss Road.

Across the road to Almshouses Lane and its worth noticing that these almshouses were erected at the request of Jacinth Sacheverell. The date on the coat of arms is 1656, thus highlighting them as among the oldest buildings around Morley.

When you reach the end of Almshouses Lane climb the stile and follow the track to The Mound. This is believed to have been a section of the pre-Roman 'Portway'. But how the mound originated remains a mystery, although some historians believe it to have been a Roman observation post. Others believe King Steven may have needed a moated and small but fortified lodge in which to defend his doubtful sovereignty against local marauders and protesters.

The track here leads to the hedgerow which, when followed, will take you down to the road. Cross with care and climb the steps and stile then turn left into Church lane. St Matthews incidentally is worth a visit. This church, with its 1400 spire and fifteenth century south chapel, has been a place of worship for both the Saxons and Normans. The magnificent stained glass windows were taken from the Abbey at Dale having been acquired by Sir Henry Sacheverell in 1539. Its brasses commemorate the life and bravery of John Sacheverell who was one of those many killed at Bosworth Field in 1485.

Walk with the church on your right, then turn left beside the graveyard. Use the beech tree as your marker and climb the stile behind it. But do not use the way-marked stile on your right. Instead cross the field diagonally left and swing to the right of the large mound, then climb the fence, turn right and climb with the track out of The Gripps.

Use as guides the marker posts that will take you across the field to the water tower. Cross from here to the hedge in front and climb the stile. While crossing these next fields note that you have the clump of trees on your left. And incidentally by the time these directions are into print, the fields may well have been transformed into a golf course, probably with markers for you to follow. Eventually you will arrive at the lane leading to the clubhouse. Cross this and climb one last stile that takes you to the main road layby and Cloves Wood.

Dependent upon your enthusiasm and the time, you could turn with the wood at your back and walk down to Morley Smithy just to have a look at the properties and retain something of the atmosphere of this interesting settlement. You will need to walk the same stretch of road back to the Cloves Wood layby.

3. Around Ockbrook

The Route: Ockbrook Moravian Settlement – Locko Park – Ockbrook Wood

Start: All Saints Church, Church Street, Ockbrook

How to Get There

By Car: From Derby or Nottingham along the A52 , situated between Spondon and Sandiacre

Parking: Car Park at the White Swan public house

Buses: Trent Services 13 and 14. (Check offices in Nottingham or Derby)

Distance: 6.5 miles

Duration: 3-4 hours

Maps: Pathfinder Series 833 – Nottingham (South West) SK43/53 1:25000

The Walk

Leaving the bus stop or car park of the White Swan, let us first wander around the churchyard while noticing the ploughshares displayed behind the silver birches in the garden alongside the pub.

The short walk along the paved path leading to the door of All Saints church is lined with yew trees. Before it became a church, All Saints was a chapel. Today only the Norman font links its origins with a pioneering era.

The spire is twelfth century and the oak chancel screen dates back to 1520, but did not become an addition until it was donated by one Thomas Pares of nearby Hopwell Hall in 1810.

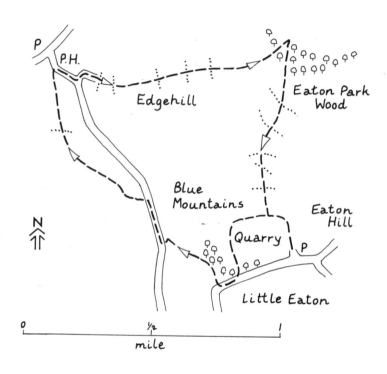

As you make your way along the church paths, notice Church Farm on your left beyond the gravestone screened wall.

On turning towards the road, look at the splendid beech tree to your left with the wide bole or trunk giving a fair indication of its age. Leave the churchyard and wall with the White Swan on your left to New Street. Fringed by a few variable houses and hawthorn and holly hedge, you can double check if you are on the correct route because Ockbrook Post Office should also be on your left.

Cross the main road by The Queens Head and the Ockbrook Studio, which specialises in antique furniture. Turn then into Bakehouse Lane. There is a gentle climb ahead with silver birches and Lombardy poplars screening one or two of the houses.

Church Farm, Ockbrook

On reaching the hilltop, bear right along the private road signposted 'The Settlement'; a few explanatory notes on which can be found at the end of this section. When you have retraced your steps to this point, take up the walk again at Grange Lodge, which should be on your right. Grange incidentally is an old English word meaning granary or grain growing farm.

Bear left now along the ridge-top. On your right is a spinney of ash and sycamore trees; on your left a house surrounded by a wall.

Take the narrow track ahead between the hedgerows to the fields you need to cross with the suburban sprawl of Spondon and the sign for Dale Road ready to catch your eye.

Turn left, then cross the road so that the shops are on your right. Your next turn should be Sancroft Road. Follow this road until you reach house number 100. From here take the path on the right with the hawthorn hedge to your left.

When you cross the farm track check that the hedge is on your right. Descend then to the foot-bridge crossing the Lees Brook which is the outflow from the lake in Locko Park.

Turn right so that you are facing oncoming traffic. Walk in single file. One sombre October morning I saw a fine fallow buck bounding from beside this roadside hedge, so from hereon start looking for small groups of fallow deer feeding in the distance.

Another swing right takes you into Locko Park. Notice the height of the oaks on either side. In the autumn rooks will be giving out their 'carr carr' calls and circling the treetops as they pluck acorns from the clusters. Other rooks you will see searching for insects with the gulls on the ploughed fields. You will probably glimpse a grey squirrel or two and pheasants searching for acorns in the leaf litter.

The trees fringing the lake are oak, alder and silver birch. Mallard, tufted duck and great crested grebe merge with the usual 'park bred' mallard and breeding pairs of Canada geese. Study as you are walking the trees across the far side for you may see a heron perched and preening.

To your right is a horse chestnut tree leaning to one side. Is this due to age or slight subterranean fault I wonder? Where the lake curves by the reeds and willows you will come to a cattle grid. Follow the path to the right with your back to the lake, but across the parkland to your left notice the fine house which is the home of the Drury-Lowe family.

There is still a family residence with the house having attracted its first occupier, Francis Smith of Warwick, in the late seventeen twenties. The Drury-Lowe's ancestors had moved in by 1774, probably soon after Frances Smith's death.

The oldest part of the complex is said to be the chapel built in 1669 and on the site, which in medieval times, provided a hospital for lepers. On your right are the fences and hurdles used in the famous Horse Trials events. At the top of the drive are the pheasant rearing pens with the bodies of shot rooks and carrion crows hanging from the wire as a warning to others of their kind, who in the season may attempt to secure both eggs and newly hatched pheasant chicks.

Once past the gamekeeper's cottage, bear left up the sand track; oak and birch scrub to the left, arable on the right. When you reach the pylon on your left, notice the slab of Bunter Sandstone which rears like an elongated spur from here to Dale Abbey.

The main road at Dunstill Cross comes as something of a surprise, so when you see the house and outbuildings on your right, that is the time to call in your children, because ahead is a fast road. Almost directly opposite the descent to the roadside, you will see a narrow track between the hawthorns and note when you reach this that the sandstone spur was obviously dynamited here to make way for the road.

For the rest of your way towards Ockbrook Wood the spur will be on your right. There are only a few yards to walk before you come to the farm gate. But you will hardly fail to notice the litter! If it is not brought by car or van, how does it get here I wonder? Beyond the gate is a farm access track. The boundary fence to the Locko Park estate is on your right. The sandstone ridge holds the boundary fence.

There is a variety of trees along the ridge; oak, beech, lime, maple, sycamore and the occasional plane.

The track turns by the outbuildings of Columbine Farm. The hedgerow should be on your left. This track takes you along the bottom boundary of Ockbrook Wood with its undulating glades and forms part of the 'Toadstool Trails' fungi foray led each October by a Derbyshire County Council Ranger.

Your route from here however is by way of the path to your right that takes you between the trees to the next stile.

You need the hedge on your right. Ahead are three fields. Take in the views as you walk towards Risley and Hopwell and down to the left those red bricked buildings are The Malthouses; derelict now and overtaken by ivy, elderberry and rosebay willow herb.

Ahead is Spots Plantation, but when you are a field's length away, you need to swing left. Make for the foot bridge that will take you along the east side of that wood (north is over your right shoulder). Oak and sycamore are predominant here. Keeping the hedge to your left, go downfield to the corner and check that you are on the right route by noting three oak trees as you pass into the next field.

Bear diagonally left to the stile. You will soon be passing, on your right, Piggin Wood, its name perhaps having derived from the days of 'pannage' when pigs were encouraged to roam free during the autumn and, like the pheasants, squirrels and deer, root for calcium enriched acorns in the leaf litter.

After climbing another stile, aim diagonally right and cross the bridge spanning a 'winterborne' stream. The next point is the stile in the hedge; before you lapwing or green plover can occasionally be seen feeding among the rooks and gulls.

Look ahead and slightly to the right. There in the elder and hawthorn hedge are two gaps. Go through either then follow the right-hand fence to the farm track. When you reach the main road, turn left and enjoy this short walk along The Ridings to All Saints Church in Ockbrook village.

The Moravian Settlement

The Settlement was founded by a group of Moravians or Czechoslovakian Protestants in 1750. The lecture hall and Sunday school on the right was used as an auxiliary hospital during the First World War.

Ockbrook School was founded in 1799 and the church dating back to 1750 is definitely worth a photograph or two. Opposite the church a letter box bears the initials GR, which tells us that it was placed there during the reign of George the Sixth, the father of our present Queen.

Where the settlement road slopes to the hill road winding to the matrix of the village, you need to turn and retrace your steps by those delightful and unusual buildings. But do pause to take in the view to your left; the Trent and Soar valleys with cooling towers of the Radcliffe on Soar power station prominent on the horizon. Proceed then to Grange Lodge which is on your right.

The Morovian Settlement, Ockbrook

4. Around Dale:
The Millers' Walk

The Route: Dale – The Flourish – Cat and Fiddle Windmill

Start: The Carpenters Arms Car Park

How to Get There

By Car: A52 from Nottingham to Spndon then A6096.

By Bus: Derby City Bus No.9, but check times and availability at Nottingham Broad Marsh or Victoria Centre

Distance: 4.5 miles

Duration: 2 to 2.5 hours

Maps: Pathfinder Series – Nottingham 833 (South West) SK43/53 1:25 000

The Walk

Having arrived at The Carpenters Arms cross the road into the village. On the right beside the Gateway Christian Centre is a footpath which you need to take while viewing the remains of the Abbey gatehouse. This was used as a jail and shelter when prisoners were being taken to Nottingham or Derby.

To the left of the garages is a garden gate. Go through this and along the path beneath the brick archway. Ahead are a small gate and stile which you need to go over and continue with the holly hedge to your left and abandoned quarry to the right.

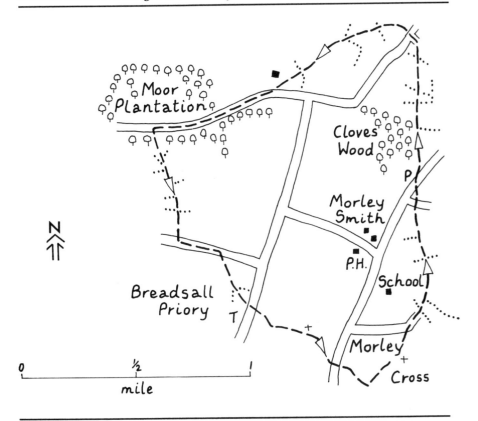

Do not use the stile on your left – but continue walking and climb the next stile. Take in now that panoramic view to your left which includes All Saints Church.

Ahead is a tree clump and you need to be passing to the right of it and then climb the stile alongside the gate. Keep the hedge to the right and go through the next two fields following the main track which leads to the fast main road.

Once across this road turn left with Flourish Farm on your right. Until 1939 this was a public house, The Stanhope Arms, which traded under a six-day licence. When the licence was not retained, the property was sold and eventually converted to a farmhouse and outbuildings. Elsewhere you find the reverse situation; a farmhouse converted to a public house.

When you reach the sign to 'Stanley', turn right and along the track to Hollies Farm. As you are passing through the yards, look for a stile beside the metal double gate. After this you walk on down the field to the next stile beside the gate beneath the power lines.

Go over the stile then bear right under the power lines to another stile and gateway. When you are over this stile check that the hedgerow is on your left and continue to the next stile which again you need to go over.

Before continuing check that the wire and post fence is on your left and locate as you are walking that old ash tree at the bottom of the field. Head for that and go over the stile beside it.

Walk then up the field and join the bridleway at Lower Hagg Farm. Then turn right in the direction of Upper Hagg Farm where a left turn into the farmyard and a few strides by the farmhouse to your right takes you to the squeeze stile and the field ahead.

Farmyards nurture, for me, a strong sense of social and agricultural history and as I'm walking I imagine the different breeds of poultry, cattle and horses that frequented those same yards and stables in the long ago.

You need to be bearing left in this field to the corner then following the track to the gate. The next field is compact and the hedge should be to your right. From the next stile you should continue along to yet another but with the hedge still on your right.

Late spring will see a variety of wild flowers flourishing here, for the meadows, thankfully, are not intensively managed.

Go over the next stile and keep the hedge to your left. Continue along the path to the main road with the Nissen type huts of the Midland Storage Depot coming into view.

A sub depot for Chilwell, this establishment specialised in the manufacture of wading and waterproof kits.

When you reach Cat and Fiddle Lane turn right and head for the A6096. To get a good view of the windmill, cross the road to the left. A paragraph or two on the mill has been included in the attached notes.

On leaving the mill, you come to a T-junction. Turn right and take the footpath signposted to the left. Go down the field with the hedge to your right. Not surprisingly another stile awaits you. After climbing it cross the path keeping the wood to your right.

Go over the next stile and swing left then follow the woodland boundary to the next stile. As you are walking I think it is worth mentioning that the wood has regenerated over the site of what was once the Dale Footrill Colliery. This was closed about forty or fifty years ago.

When you reach the farm buildings turn right. The footbridge and stile are close to the oak tree and beyond them a track leading across the field to the main road. Your starting point at Dale is along on the right.

The Cat and Fiddle Windmill

Built in the eighteenth century this is a 'post mill', a term distinguishable by the fact that the superstructure housing is mounted on an upright wooden post.

The Roundhouse is made from stone. At intervals the sails are removed for refurbishment, but the entire structure provides a clean cut and interesting landmark especially when viewed from a distance.

5. Around Dale Abbey: The Hermit's Walk

The Route: Pioneer Meadows – Furnace Road Farm – Hermit's Wood – Dale Abbey

Start: Pioneer Meadows off Wirksworth Road, Kirk Hallam, Ilkeston

How to Get There

By Car: A52 from Nottingham to Spondon A6096

Parking: Pioneer Meadows Car Park

By Bus: Barton 4A, 51 and 53. Trent 52, or 19 from Derby to St Norberts Drive, Kirk Hallam, but check at Nottingham or Derby bus station.

Distance: 3.25 miles

Duration: 2.5 hours

Maps: Pathfinder Series 833 – Nottingham South West SK43/53 1:25 000

The Walk

Pioneer Meadows has a car park. The grassland has been designated as a Public Open Space and in the season nurtures such wild flower species as the lady's smock, ragged robin and toadflax.

From the nearby gate take the centre of the three surfaced paths and over the bridge crossing the Sow Brook. Turn right then and proceed along the edge of the first field and into the next.

When you are two-thirds along this field the path bears left. Cross the stile and head for the pylon with the intention of passing to the right of it. But do not cross the stream. Instead follow the path to the right and cross the chipping littered track of the former mineral railway.

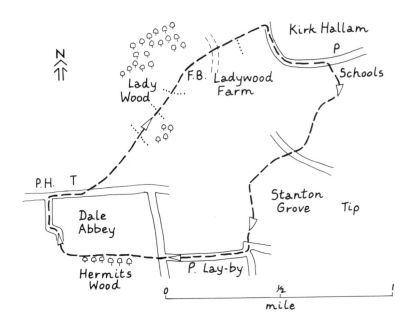

This is a good place for locating small bird species, especially summer visitors like the chiff chaff, grasshopper warbler and willow warbler.

The mineral line linked Stanton Ironworks with the two collieries at Dale, a sand quarry and nearby group of clay pits, so it was well and truly productive in its day. Having crossed, follow the hedge to the next stile and cross the field; heading for its far corner. Bear left through the gate and follow the path to Furnace Pond, so-called because it powered the water-driven bellows that were part of the blast furnace complex which was in operation here during eighteenth century. The farm and cottages are worth a photograph.

Leave the pond by the surfaced track that connects with the junction of Hixons Lane. Now turn right and with care follow Dale Road, noticing about half-way along the spires of Ilkeston's United Reform Church and St Mary's Church and the conspicuously sited Cat and Fiddle Windmill.

Dale Road meets with the junction of Woodpecker Hill and Potato Pit Lane. Cross the road and go through the field gate, then bear slightly to the right of the wood for you are on the bridle road to Dale. The path leading through Hermits Wood winds away from the far corner of the field. Although long regarded as a public place, the Hermits Cave in the sandstone abutment to your left is listed as a 'concessionary public access', meaning that if the site were abused the landowner could close it off.

Hermits Wood is rightly termed 'ancient'. The shrub layer attracts all the usual woodland bird species and small mammals. An occasional fox may also be glimpsed. The trees are ash, oak, lime and beech. The wild flowers, ramson, bluebells, wood anemones and yellow archangel.

The Hermit's Cave can be reached by taking the flight of sandstone steps to your left. The hermit, a Derby baker, arrived here around the year 1130 after claiming to have seen a vision of the Virgin Mary. He hewed

The Hermit's Cave

and carved the cave out of the sandstone and, at the front, built a lean-to for himself and his livestock. Nearby Dale Abbey and its church were built twenty years or so later, for the alleged Virginal Vision proclaimed 'Depedale' as Dale was then known a holy place.

Leaving the cave and returning to the bridleway with the fields to your right, go through the gate and bear right through the yard of Church Farm, with its cheery and enthusiastic young equestrians, and stile to the right. This takes you into the field where, by bearing left, you can view the Dale Abbey Arch, which was the great east window of a building around which was spread some 24,000 acres of land.

The Abbey of St Marys, as the place of worship was known, would have appeared magnificent rising against its background of the surrounding forest. The existing arched window frame stands forty feet in height, which gives us a fair idea of the size and proportions of the building. The Abbey suffered the fate of dissolution in 1538.

When you return to the village street, turn right and you will see that one or two of the firm walled cottages have been built from the Abbey stones. Take note too of All Saints Church by your right shoulder there. It was built first as a church then became a farmhouse. But I should add that it has also been used as a pub, and if I'm not mistaken a delicious cup of coffee can still provide that welcome break on Sunday afternoons.

Make your way now along to the Carpenters Arms, noticing on your left the seat donated by the villagers and the beautifully converted barn.

If you turn left, just as a diversion, you will come to a tubular gate. Walk into this field and upslope a little to your right. Below are the row of cottages but look at the one nearest to the field. Usually the beautifully tended garden of this – Mayfield Cottage – looks superb. Return then to the main street and turn left for the described route.

Dependent upon the hour, the Carpenters Arms will provide you with that small room atmosphere, which today is sadly lacking in many country pubs. And if you are teetotal, I think you'll agree that the pub front with its masses of wall screening vine enhances the roadside scene.

But to continue the walk, you need to turn right and past the old school, looking for and entering the second field on your left. Bear right across the field towards the barns in the next field – cross the footbridge then walk alongside the hedge, but ignore the path beside the wood. At the power lines bear left, go over the next stile then turn right and follow the hedgerow. This route was part of the former Stanton Dale tramway which fell into disrepair at the beginning of this century. Today the bustle of activity that must have taken place around here seems hardly credible.

Cross two more fields and you should be crossing the bridge and taking the path beside Ladywood Farm noticing the interesting buildings and perhaps thinking again of times gone by.

Continue along the hillbrow and join Kirk Hallam near the small recreation ground. A fine right turn and you are on the last leg of your walk and hopefully heading towards nearby Pioneer Meadows.

6. Around West Hallam: The Miner's Walk

The Route: White Hart – Briggswood Farm – Hayes Park Farm – The Gripps – Morley – Stanley Village

Start: Community Centre, Station Road, West Hallam or, with the landlord's consent, parking in the car park of The White Hart, West Hallam

How to Get There

By Car: From Nottingham: take the Wollaton-Trowell Road A609, and follow through Ilkeston turning left on High Lane. From Derby: A608 turning right onto the A609.

By Bus: 120 Trent – 12 Felix. Do check timetables before setting out.

Distance: 5 miles

Duration: 2.5 – 3 hours

Maps: Pathfinder Series – Nottingham/North and Ilkeston SK44/54 and Belper SK24/34

The Walk

Leave the West Hallam Community Centre by turning left, crossing the road and taking the first turn on the right which is Bagot Street.

On the sharp right-hand bend is a path by the White Hart public house and a signpost to 'Stanley'. Turn here with the public house to your right. While you are in the White Hart car park, stand with your back to the stables. On the other side of the nearside hedge is a sand track leading off from the main road. Walk to this, pass through one of the several hedgegaps, then turn right. This is the beginning of your walk.

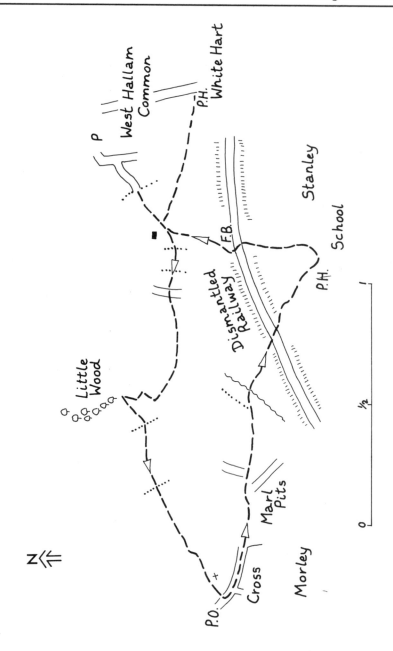

Notice the splendid oaks in the hedgerow here. These were probably planted as field boundary markers. Smaller, self regenerated oaks alternate alongside stands of hawthorn. Crossing the stile at the tubular gate, pause to admire the views of the surrounding countryside. On the right, beyond the hedge, are several paddocks of long grass over which a barn owl or short eared owl may be seen hunting on late winter afternoons.

Between the two pylons up ahead is an oak which, from the photographic point of view, provides an interesting silhouette for the sun sets directly behind it. Notice the deep tangles of blackberry thicket and in the long grasses beside the hedge the occasional 'form' or resting place used by a hare or fox.

The gate of the paddock on the right carries a notice requesting footpath walkers not to feed the horses. That singular tree on the far side of the paddock is a Lombardy poplar.

When you reach the corner of the field turn left and look at the view along the opposite ridge. Take in the various shapes of the fields and remember that a hundred or so years ago each field was given a name.

You should have turned so that the pylon is in front of you. Follow the hedgeline to your right, pass beneath the pylon, and take another look at the view. The Cat and Fiddle Windmill stands out clearly from here. Stanley village sprawls to the south and south west, while Stanley Common extends northwards.

At the next stile notice the mass of thistles growing in the nearest corner of the field. Many small birds and especially 'chimes' of goldfinches will feed on those seed heads. With the hedge on your left, make your way up to the next field in the direction of the tall ash tree by the stile. It is quite likely that you will put up a 'covey' of partridges and at dusk you may well hear their rusty calls as the birds assemble to roost on the ground, each with its head facing outwards.

Notice how the old stone drinking trough over to your right has been positioned close to the oak. Here the cattle can find both shade and water. One day I came across the body of a hedgehog on the field slope; its death grimace suggesting that it had probably been trampled by curious cows.

At the ash tree stile pause and look back. On a clear day you can see the distant hills of Charnwood Forest in Leicestershire. Having crossed the stile you should be walking with the hedgerow to your left noticing perhaps another stone trough in the single hedgegap.

To the right of the next stile, which you need to climb, is a holly hedge. Pause before following the hedgeline for you will see a succession of mounds in the field, which have me exploring the possibility of there having been a settlement here, though what date we could put alongside it is difficult to determine.

The garden of Briggswood Farm should be to your right as you follow the field boundary to Common Lane. The hedgerow supports a surprising variety of trees among them being the hawthorn, holly, blackthorn, crab apple and field maple. Having crossed Common Lane and climbed the stile in the corner of the field, proceed across two further fields keeping the hedgerow on your right. The spire of Morley Church begins to peer above the horizon.

In the summer these relatively untended meadows provide anchorage for many wild flowers, with camomile and poppies being the most prominent.

Ahead a stile beckons, after which you go to the bridge crossing the Stanley Brook. Cross the bridge continue over two more fields until the path meets with a cart track. Park Farm is over to your left. But you need to turn right and walk to the gateway on your left by the telegraph poles.

Pass through the gateway with the hedge on your right as you make for the near corner of Little Wood; and try to imagine if you can the local colliers of a hundred years ago collecting kindle or putting out a snare to catch one of the many rabbits.

Turn now and walk back up the field. You need to be looking at the second telegraph pole at which you turn right and follow the telegraph lines with the intention of reaching the hedge on your right. Look at the tops of the telegraph poles, especially those ahead, for you may see a kestrel or little owl perched and scanning for prey.

Follow the hedge to the next stile and still with the hedge on your right continue to the brook, cross it then begin the steady climb towards Morley church spire.

You should be heading for the left corner of the enclosure then bearing left and crossing the stile into a wooded valley, for long known as The Gripps. Take the descending path to the right, then cross the stream. Continue uphill towards the church spire. Having then arrived at the brow of the hill, look to your right for the stile in the corner of the stone wall. The stile you need next is in the left corner of the field. The churchyard wall should be on your left because you are looking for the kissing gate and the church drive beyond.

Morley Church incidentally bears evidence of both Saxon and Norman interest. But the local people rightfully highlight the stained glass windows taken originally from the Abbey Refectory at Dale where they were acquired by Sir Henry Sackeverrell in 1539.

Church Drive leads you onto the main road where with care you should turn left, proceed around the sharp bend, then head up the hill marked 'No Through Road' – This sign is intended for motorists.

On the right are two picturesque ponds from which marl was extracted in bygone times. Tenanted by moorhens, they deserve a photograph, while respecting also the notice showing that the land is 'Private'. Continue along the lane with its interesting and varied properties surrounded by well maintained gardens. Where the gate crosses the lane your route winds beyond it, keeping the hedgerow to your right until a line of willows dominating the fewer oaks and ash show the field boundary bordered by the Stanley Brook.

On the map, the crossing at the next gateway is described as a 'Ford', but both steps and a wooden footbridge have been added to aid the walker who may be advanced in years. The path follows the hedgeline which should be on your right. Notice over to your left, the ruins of what may have been a small barn or stockman's cottage. In the early part of this century, many Midland farms preferred to house their stock keeping staff on the very fields grazed by cattle and sheep.

The field sweeps gently toward the skyline. Up ahead is another gate. After passing through this continue along the track for a few yards between a paddock grazing goats to your left and garden plots filled in the season with cabbages to your right.

Here the track joins Morley Lane and you should be crossing the bridge of the disused railway. Turn right after crossing the bridge with White House Farm on your right. Beyond the houses and outbuildings are several interesting paddocks and further along the road you will notice how the oak and sycamore branches meet to form an arch.

Common Lane joins Morley Lane at a narrow bend and you need to keep to the latter. On your right is a house surrounded by yew trees with branches almost reaching to the roof. There is also a fine cedar here and by the side door a two wheeled farm cart, soil filled and planted with flowers. How old is the house and outbuildings of Stanley Farm, I wonder; the next cluster of buildings to your right? And notice the contrasts for after the farm house are a number of modern and converted houses set back off the road with a Porsche or BMW parked in every other driveway.

When you reach the Derby Road junction bear slightly left and take the right-hand bend. The stand of beech trees makes a change from the oaks and hollies. You will pass a war memorial and church. Begin looking then for the cedar shading the house, named not surprisingly 'The Cedars'.

Having reached this, notice that the road takes another, more severe, right-hand bend, then look to your left for the sign pointing towards two rows of houses. Cross the road to the sign. It should bear the words 'To Stanley Common'.

Walk the narrow track extending the length of the gardens then pass through the hand gate. A sportsfield with football pitches included should be on your right. Follow the hedgeline and top the stile so that again you meet with the disused railway. If you have the time to pause here a while, then turn to the explanatory piece at the end of the walk.

Beyond the railway you will need to keep the hedge on your right and will have no doubt recognised the pylon. All you need to do now is follow the footpath and hedgeline back up the fields to the sand track. Turn right and, within the next hundred or so yards, you will be back in the car park of the White Hart – and do bear in mind the menu with its delicious homemade soup! From the White Hart, turn left along Station Road to the Community Centre.

The Disused Railway

By way of a diversion you could take one of the stairway-type paths down the embankment and explore the disused railway. But this is not a route recommended for wet weather walking due to the enmeshing vegetation.

Having said that, under favourable conditions this is the type of place where, if you sit quietly at a vantage point, you will see more wild life species in half an hour than you would walking for four hours.

The trees thriving between the embankments are hawthorn, blackthorn, silver birch, maple, sycamore and oak. Consequently in the autumn, grey squirrels, pheasants and jays will be foraging for acorns, sloes and haw berries. All of the trees are self regenerated as are the grasses and stands of bramble, elder and rosebay willow herb.

Linnets and bullfinches will visit such wealthy habitats daily and the winter months should see redwings and fieldfares plucking the haw berries. Sparrowhawk and kestrel hunt here and I have one memorable sequence of a kestrel pursuing small birds against the background of a late autumn sunset.

The actual railway line was the Great Northern Derbyshire extension of 1878 which connected Derby Friargate station with Nottingham Victoria. On the 6th May 1968 the line was closed and the track removed the following year.

The track today is a definitive right of way owned by the Derbyshire County Council who supported the local community in their successful attempt to thwart the threat of an opencast mining development when coal seams were discovered some ten feet below ground.

7. Exploring the Nutbrook Canal

The Route: Manners Floods – Kirk Hallam Lake – Godfrey Drive – Nutbrook Canal – Stanton – Return

Start: Car Park by Kirk Hallam School, Pioneer Meadows

How to Get There

By Car: To Ilkeston, then take the A609 downhill and over railway bridge. Where the road bends and there is a sheet of water on the right, turn sharp left and along the 15 mph lane to the car park.

Buses: Trent 235 or 51 Broad Marsh – check times at 'Enquiries' office. Alight Kirk Hallam School and walk with the lake on your left round to the bridge and path to car park on the far side.

Duration: 2.5 – 3 hours

Distance: 3.5 to 4 miles

Maps: Nottingham North and Ilkeston – Sheet SK44/54 Pathfinder 812 and O/S Pathfinder 833 (Sheets SK43/53) Nottingham South West.

The Walk: route 1

To begin this walk, turn left from the car park ensuring that the hawthorn scrubland is to your left and the recreation field on your right. The motorists are of course walking the road down which they have just driven. Hawthorn and oaks are prolific on your left, a few with ivy entwined trunks and if you happen along that way on a mid-week evening, then the bonus could be attempting to keep in step with one of the several local brass bands which rehearse on the recreation field.

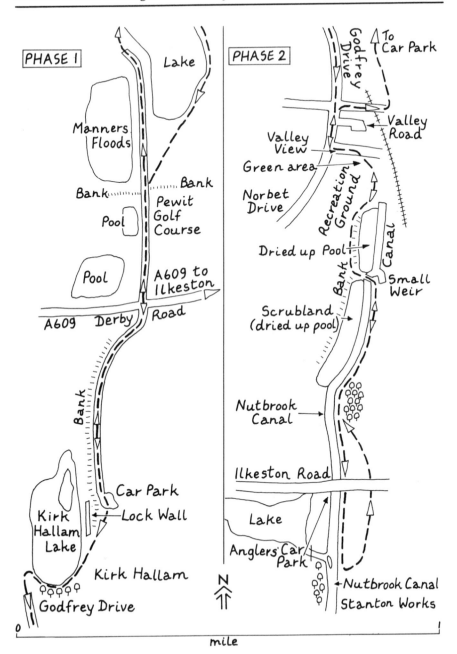

When you see the line of willows on your left you are nearing the main road and should check on the children or family dog if they are running ahead. Cross the road on the bend and notice the sheet of water to your left as you are about to go through the hand gate. This usually attracts six or eight non-breeding mute swans in to feed and also diving ducks like the tufted and pochard.

Continue along the track between the willow and bramble thickets to the railway bridge where it is worth pausing to admire the graffiti type artwork, or collages, the local youths have produced to enhance the otherwise sombre brickwork either side of the bridge. Like most environmentalists, I'm never in favour of blatantly glaring graffiti, but displayed here it is colourful and inoffensive.

As you are leaving the bridge you will notice a pool beyond the hedge to your left. The small overgrown tract of ground between the two water courses is worth investigating during the summer, when such wild flower species as toadflax, meadow cranesbill and camomile provide more welcome colour within the myriads of meadow buttercup.

If you look around here then your next step is to return to the path with your back to the railway and continue along the track. Joining the oaks and willows along the brook bank to your left are strands of gorse and broom. Notice the golf course on your right sloping down to this semi-wild area that nurtures both plants and wildlife. Continue up the steep bank and as you are descending notice the different stages of reed growth colonising the lake surface to your left.

If you are walking in April you may see the unusual sight of two mute swans each sitting a nest situated about a hundred yards apart. I stress that word unusual, because mute swans are territorial and only one pair would normally occupy a stretch of water this size. I have however included a few paragraphs on these interesting birds at the end of this section.

Those dead alders serve as perches for the occasional heron, carrion crow or kestrel. The reed beds are summer roosts for swallows and martins, or winter roosts for starlings.

Just ahead on your right is a lake. Follow the lake path around to the far side and back to the culvert by the reedy pool holding the dead alders. Then continue along the track and over the main road to the car park for the second phase of this explorative ramble.

The Walk: route 2

Adjacent to the car park, but off to the right, is a bridge crossing the brook. Cross this to the lake with the island, anglers and mute swans.

Turn left with the lake on your right, but look along the bank to your left for here alongside three dilapidated seats you will see the stone walling of a bygone lock gate.

This was Lock Number Five; known to the canal people as 'Bottom of Three' or 'Oxmeadow Lock'; the latter name suggests that during medieval times oxen grazed the area that today is a lake, school and housing estate.

The lake here originated as a means of controlling the surplus water which had formed within the nearby canal pounds – as the stretch of water between each set of lock gates was known. Yet other than the stones there is little indication that the canal extended this far.

When you turn with the lake path have the belt of poplar trees on your right. At the crossroads turn left onto Godfrey Drive and proceed by the houses and gardens. Satellite dish country this, but there are several well-tended gardens to divert your gaze from the brickwork.

At the next set of crossroads you will see, when you cross directly ahead, a group of old people's bungalows and Valley Road with a green area and a fine ash tree by the houses on the far side of the road.

But you need to be on the left keeping the equally fine oak tree on your right. Turn then into Valley View and cross with the sports area on your right. Once on the grass, keep left so that you are rounding the edge of the sports field, keeping the trough of scrub oak, willow and hawthorn to your left and the recreation area to your right.

Eventually you will see the reeds which remind the locals that this was the original bed of the Nutbrook Canal. Where the scrub area widens and deepens, take the grass path to your left and cross the rusty railed bridge over the canal. The Nutbrook itself cascades down the weir sills to form a narrower channel behind the hawthorn thickets. Turn right and along the towpath that will take you down to the Stanton reach and, although you need to come back this way, it is well worth the walk.

Keep your eye on the overhanging tree branches because kingfishers are not unknown along with reed buntings and pied wagtails.

Beyond the disused lock gate and dam wall is a fast main road, so take care. Feed the mute swan pair from the towpath or anglers' car park on the opposite bank. Behind the reedy angular island on your left is a channel which connects the canal to the private lake. A plank bridge crosses this channel and you might feel inclined to walk the paths threaded between the wooded banks.

The glades will provide glimpses of the canal on one side and private lake the other. You will eventually have to retrace your steps to the car park, cross the main road and return to Park Avenue by way of the towpath.

But for a rough walk diversion you can turn from the towpath and wander through the willow scrub towards the road. In the early morning and at dusk a colony of rabbits feeds here. You might glimpse a fox. And usually there are finches and titmice flying around the thickets.

When you have crossed the fast road with Stanton Ironworks at your back, climb the fence and walk the rough tussocky field between the hedgerows, where an occasional barn owl hunts or herons become disturbed as they fly in to catch fish or small mammals along the canal. By bearing left you will eventually meet with the canal towpath and the weir on your right.

Here you need to cross the rusted bridge and retrace your steps to the crossroads. But this time, if you have adequate footwear, turn right, cross the road, go over the railway bridge and turn immediately left down the steps and onto the derelict mineral railway line.

The willows over to your right screen a bygone boating lake called The Beauty Spot, a name which many local folk regard as a misnomer. You will not thank me for having led you over ground littered with loose chippings, but tread carefully.

Within a few hundred yards you will see the school playing fields between the thickets to your left. Take any one of the several gaps in the hedge and enter the open area. Swing half right and make as if towards the farthest corner of the grass and eventually the car park comes into view.

The bus passenger can then either cross the bridge and walk around a section of the lake beyond to a bus stop, or carry on along the lane to Straws Bridge and the bus stops appropriately signposted nearby.

The Nutbrook Canal

The Nutbrook Canal was built as a short cut from Shipley Gate, through the Nutbrook Valley to Dale Ironworks. It was the brain-child of Edward Miller Mundy who was dissatisfied with the transportation of his coals along the Erewash Canal.

A decade or so elapsed before the actual proposal for this waterway was put forward and work was not begun until 1791. It took five years to complete the four and a half mile route which provided employment for three lock keepers and of course the bargees and their families.

The main problem with this private venture was leakage, consequently Miller Mundy decided to have a dam built across the coaching drive to Shipley Hall. By doing this he saw the double advantage of having an ornamental sheet of water before the Halls windows and ensuring that a ready water supply was available to flood the canal pounds should serious leakage problems arise.

Additional water was channelled from the brook which fed Hawley's Pond and in 1821 Mapperley Reservoir was built to reinforce the canal's existence.

After serving its purpose for fifty years, the Nutbrook Canal faced the threat of coal mining for the workings of the Butterley and Potter

Colliery threaded directly beneath the waterway. Miller Mundy, in 1854, decided to extract coal from beneath Mapperley Reservoir and the feared and final leaks occurred in 1867 flooding the Butterley and Potter Mines beneath West Hallam.

Some years later the canal was replaced by the railway linking the Shipley collieries with the Erewash Canal. Thus the canal was closed, but managed by two companies assigned to Shipley Collieries Limited.

The Stanton end however was still used by the Stanton Ironworks Company to route their traffic along the Erewash Canal to the River Trent. But by 1949 the waterway was termed 'disused' and became colonised by aquatic plans, amphibians, birds and small mammals.

The Nutbrook Mute Swans

The two rival pairs of mute swans currently breeding in this area are interesting in that they are not typical of the bird enthusiast's basic image.

The pair holding a territory on the Stanton stretch of the canal and its adjacent lake are typical from the size viewpoint in that the male or 'cob' is considerably larger than the female or 'pen'. In most pairs however the cob carries the largest black knob or 'berry' surmounting the base of the bill. This pair are different for it is the pen which carries a more prominent berry than her mate.

The Stanton cob and pen have been together since the late Sixties and have bred on the original Shipley Park Lake, Loscoe Dam and the Erewash Canal before adopting their present territory.

Most years they nest on the triangular islet where the canal channel meets the lake. With their cygnets in tow they often walk across the car park waiting for bread to be thrown, but fortunately one or two knowing folk have begun bringing them grain which is beneficial to swans and most birds that readily accept 'handouts' from kindly humans.

The Manner Floods' swans are exceptional due to the fact that they are a breeding trio consisting of one cob and two pens. The cob arrived on the midsummer moulting area of the Attenborough Reserve in 1975 and after leaving in the autumn returned the following summer.

A four or five year old bird, he was back a year later and easily identifiable by the pale Darvic Ring attached to the right leg which carries the letters 'E B'. By 1979 this cob had acquired a mate and the pair first bred on the lake by the Kirk Hallam school, but vacated the site for nearby Manner Floods, which is a more natural water. And here they annually reared a brood of five or six cygnets. However in April 1990 several interested local observers noticed E B mating with and building nests for two females.

The Newcomer 'pen' is a considerably younger bird and I have not overlooked the possibility of it being one of their offspring, for quite often a pair will keep a favoured female cygnet with them throughout the winter months. In this instance the 'parental bond' may have developed beyond the natural theme.

Mute swan pair at Kirk Hallam. Notice that the nearest bird, the male 'cob' is larger and higher than the female 'pen'

In 1990 both pens hatched off a brood of cygnets, but the Newcomer and her cygnets were driven onto the recreational lake where they remained until the following breeding season. 1991 saw the original pen disturbed from her eggs and E B escorting the Newcomer and their brood of three.

By May 1992 the situation had reversed and the original pen brought off six cygnets, although whether one or two were the Newcomer's is difficult to define, since this pen was alone on the recreational lake soon after the original pair reformed with their own brood. Meanwhile, the cob, E B remains the mate of both.

The Erewash Valley

Rising just south of Kirkby in Ashfield the River Erewash swings west before turning towards Pinxton and continuing along the western edge of Nottinghamshire, where for some distance the waterway constitutes the boundary between the two counties.

The water source surges over magnesium limestone, but channels eventually between banks of shale and clay. It is not the most scenic river in the region, although the name Erewash in Old English means 'winding stream', which suggests that the original source still exists, but only around Pinxton and Ilkeston. From there on it appears to have been straightened, particularly throughout Toton and Long Eaton and probably when the canal and railway companies were getting established and wharfs or loading bays needed to be free from the threat of flooding. The river enters the Trent half a mile or so below Toton Arches on the A453 and close to the Long Eaton boundary.

The valley today interprets the remains of a once-thriving coalfield heavily disguised by derelict land, industrial sites, urban development, hamlets and attractive villages.

There are still miles of hedgerow, acres of unspoilt pasture land and pockets of regenerated woodland where scrub and secondary thicket have taken hold. The coal mining developments of the past were extensive. although over the past forty years open cast extraction has taken place. Fortunately the farmland has escaped intense management. Consequently the grasslands support a variety of wild flowers on both acidic and neutral soils with orchids still thriving in the limestone grasslands around Pinxton and Kirkby in Ashfield.

In the cluttered towns, like Long Eaton and Ilkeston, one gains an awareness of recreational areas expanding alongside industrial development and all forms of sport and leisure activities take place throughout the region.

To make everyone aware of these facilities, the Borough of Erewash Council publish an annual called 'Erewash Leisure'. This can be obtained from the town hall, sports and leisure offices, libraries or newsagents.

Close to Ilkeston Market Place on High Street is the Erewash Museum, a listed Grade II late eighteenth century house, which served first as a family home and later a school, until it was converted into a social life museum in the early nineteen eighties.

Though small, the informal walled garden retains a sense of peace and the museum is compact with a friendly staff. Among the local history exhibits is a scullery reconstructed from a terraced house in Cotmanhay and I have it on good authority that the coffee served at the museum on Thursday afternoon only is 'the best for miles around'.

On going to press the museum opens from October to March on Thursday and Friday only (10.00 a.m. – 12 noon and 1.00 p.m. – 4.00 p.m.). From April to September this schedule is extended to include Saturday. The times are the same; but arrangements can be made to view at other times. The enquirer should phone 440440 Ext:331; if possible, well ahead of their intended visit.

Mention should also be made of the excellent work of the Erewash Groundwork Trust, a team of Conservation Volunteers and active in the restoration of wild flower meadows and derelict ponds, planting trees, clearing ditches etc. Anyone wishing to help or learn more should contact:

Erewash Groundwork Trust 43 Town Street Sandiacre Nottingham NG10 5DU Tel: (0602) 490235

8. Around Breaston and Draycott: The Coffin Bearers' Walk

The Route: Breaston – Wilne Cross – Derwent Flood Bank – Nooning Lane – Cottage Farm

Start: St. Michael's Church, Main Street Breaston

How to Get There

By Car: From Nottingham to Long Eaton then A6005 signposted on the right. From Derby – A52 or A6005

Parking: Car Park opposite St Michael's Church

By Bus: Trent: Services 5, 5B and 5C – check times at Nottingham or Derby Bus Station

Distance: 5 miles

Duration: 2.5 – 3 hours

Maps: Pathfinder Series 833/Nottingham/South West SK43/53 1:25 000

This easy and interesting walk begins at the car park opposite Breaston Church. Dating from the 13th century, St Michael's was originally a chapel. Related events such as funerals, weddings and baptisms were conducted at St Chad's Church, Wilne, which entailed a short walk, coach or horse ride south of the relatively outlying villages of Breaston and Draycott.

Breaston and Draycott

To many local people, the most significant building in Draycott is that housing the Victoria Mills and currently the business premises of the electrical component manufacturers J H Parry. Built between 1888 and 1907 these four-storey tenements were prolific in the manufacture of lace, a product which would have provided quite a number of local households with a satisfactory income in times gone by. One impressive feature is the green capped clock tower which furnishes the entire building with an aspect of localised individuality.

Although a short distance from Draycott the church of St Chad at Wilne was at one time destroyed by fire. The font is thought to be one of the oldest in the country, constructed by a pre-Norman cross shaft turned completely about. The effigies depict members of the Willoughby family and panes of glass in the windows date back to the Renaissance period.

Breaston's thriving community has probably to do with the fact that the village is situated midway between Nottingham and Derby.

St Michael's is a fourteenth century church but with several interesting period renovations. If you happen to be wandering in the graveyards hereabouts, you may come across the name Astil carved on one or two of the gravestones. The original name however was Easthill – 'people of the East Hill'; a point used to illustrate how many such names have been changed throughout the last two or three centuries.

The Astils incidentally were cotton and lace manufacturers. One of their mills beside the Derwent at Church Wilne has long since been converted into the firework factory, which has continued trading throughout a series of national recessions.

The Walk

First you need to walk down Church View then climb the stile and turn right. With the hedge on your right, take the direction indicated by the sign; climb the next stile and the next. Here the fence should be on your right.

Cross now the next field but diagonally to the two step stile then follow the garden fence and climb the next stile. Ahead is the bridge over the stream and the railway line both of which you need to cross; the latter of course with care.

Another example of the ridge and furrow system can be seen on the field to the right, which grazes the ponies of The Pony Rescue Centre. To the left opposite the gate to this Centre are the Coffin Stones where the

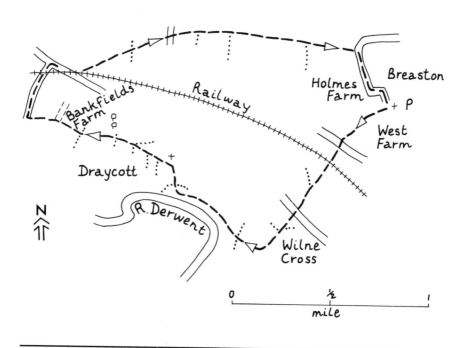

coffins were laid when the bearers needed a rest when a burial was to take place at Wilne.

The track leads then to Wilne Cross on Sawley Road. Cross to the bridleway and continue to the stile on your right. After climbing it follow the floodbank path with the River Derwent on your left.

You pass a small section of the sixty mile watercourse here, the Derwent having surfaced at Ronksley Moor, Bleaklow and meandered between contours of limestone and grit to join the Trent at an attractive point between Sawley and Wilne. The Derwent is not a navigable river therefore fish and amphibians thrive below its surface and several waterbird species above.

You may flush mallard, tufted and pochard duck. Coot, moorhens, mute swans and a variety of gulls will be more tolerant, although your silhouette will disturb little grebe and herons.

A row of poplar trees should be on your right as you continue along the floodbank to the road, which you should cross, then proceed along the floodbank to those white painted cottages on your right.

Climb the stile here and head directly into Draycott. A left turn will take you into Derwent Street along which there is a footpath sign and here you should turn right and continue through the housing estate, but turning left just before you reach Queens Court. Follow the road then turn left into Lime Grove. Continue by the open stretch to the snicket on the bend. Turn then into the snicket and continue to the stile, then cross a field with the small wood on your right.

At the next stile and to your right is Bankfield Farm, then swing right towards the willows. The fields will take you to Nooning Lane, providing the hedge and fence are on your left. Here on the lane turn right and walk to the main road where you should turn right again, cross the road and before you reach the railway bridge turn onto the footpath to your left.

You are now following the line of the Derby Canal, built by Benjamin Outram and opened in 1798. Its barges transported quarried stone, agricultural crops, coal and later the sleepers and rails for the railways which put it out of business. Notice too, the aqueduct. The canal was abandoned during the Second World War and very little trace of it remains, although I have friends approaching the age of fifty, who can recall towpaths bright with wild flowers and butterflies and the occasional glimpse of a kingfisher.

This canal route leads towards Fields Farm when you reach Hopwell Road, then cross and continue along the footpath opposite alongside a plantation.

Continue over two stiles and at the track near Cottage Farm, climb the stile and turn right using the church spire ahead as your pointer back along the road to the car park.

Look out for the Little Owls!

If you choose to leave your Erewash walk locations via Rushy Lane, which connects Stanton by Dale with Sandiacre or Risley, look for the little owls that appear as small figure of eight shapes, either on the top of a telegraph post or perched along the wires.

About one and a half times again bigger than a house sparrow, the Little Owl was introduced from Holland into Northamptonshire by Lord Lilford around the turn of the century.

Little owls are diurnal, which means that they hunt in both daylight and darkness. The telegraph poles hereabouts are used for scanning prey. This comprises virtually anything smaller than the bird; insects, cockchafers, small birds and mammals etc. The widespread breeding pairs nest in derelict farm and colliery buildings, hollow trees, or disused rabbit burrows.

9. Around Sandiacre

The Route: Stoney Clouds – Stanton by Dale – Peatmeadow Farm – Sandiacre

Start: Sandiacre Library car park, off Doncaster Avenue or car park of The Plough with the landlord's consent.

How to Get There

By Car: From Derby A52 to Borrowash then B5010. From Nottingham A52 and B5010.

By Bus: Barton: Services 4 – 4A and 17, Trent 102. Check timetables at Nottingham or Derby.

Distance: 6 miles

Duration: 2.5 – 3 hours

Maps: Pathfinder Series 833 – Nottingham (South West) SK43/53 1:25 000

The Walk

From the Sandiacre Library car park head across the recreation ground and turn right into Kings Road. Beside the bus stop to Stanton road is a jitty on your left. Use this merely as a guide marker because you need then to turn right, cross the road, take the first turn on the left, turn left again and ahead should be the hill leading to St Giles Church.

Notice the holly trees clustered and the steep overgrown banks and the cow sign at the head of the track leading to Church Farm.

St Giles parish is locally admired for its architecture. Parts of the building date to the tenth century. The chancel arch has two distinguishing features; the 'Sandiacre Imp' carved on the actual arch and the Saxon window above it. On leaving the church, keep straight

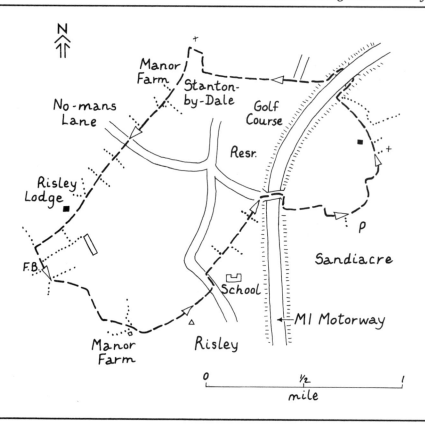

ahead by the houses and laneside banks flanked by ash, sycamore and ground ivy. At the lane's end climb the stile by the farm gate and you are on to an area designated as Public Open Space and known as 'Cloudside', due to the sandstone outcrop which our walking ancestors called 'Stoney Clouds'.

But they could hardly have failed to notice the signs of the medieval crop rotation programme which was known as The Ridge and Furrow. This is a fine example of the remains of medieval farming and, because the grassland is unmanaged, quite a number of wild flower species can be identified when you are walking in the summer. Moles also thrive here and you are bound to come across their many spoil piles or 'heaps'.

Down below to the right, the Ridge and Furrow system is still prevalent despite the golf course and no doubt when you see the motorway you will be wondering how many vehicles pass by in the space of an hour.

Over to your left among the brambles and scrub oak is a marker post. This guides you between the sandstone banks where gorse and bracken have also taken hold.

Having descended to the level of the motorway, climb the next stile and turn right with the motorway to your left. Over your right shoulder you can gain another aspect of The Clouds you have just descended.

Ahead beyond the motorway and the housing and industrial sprawl you will see two wooded ridges known as Stapleford Hill and Bramcote Woods respectively. These sites are also designated as public open spaces with several interesting paths threading between the trees and quarry banks.

Familiar landmark on the ridge between Stanton-by-Dale and Sandiacre

Walk along the edge of the golf course to the tunnel which takes you under the motorway. On the other side climb the stile, then swing left with the M1 now on your left.

Follow the white markers which eventually lead you across the width of the golf course over the Ridge and Furrows, noticing perhaps the many young trees that have been planted, such as silver birch, black poplar, maple and sycamore.

Most of the people in Stanton by Dale are very friendly and the golf club members here are no exception. They make you feel welcome rather than suggest that you are trespassing and I cannot say the same for every golf course I've crossed! When you reach the gate by the walled road, turn left and keep an eye out for the grey squirrels that frequent the pleasant stands of oak and sycamore. Quite often these rodents will cross the road to feed in the small mixed wood to your right; while those ivy clad trunks of the pine trees on your left were probably scaled regularly by our native red squirrels until some forty or fifty years ago.

For the photographer I should mention the fact that some interesting silhouettes of golfing groups and trees can be obtained along here, especially where the golf course rises slightly higher than the road.

In the valley off to the right is the not so pretty sprawl of Stanton Works, from which this village Stanton by Dale gets its name. Not surprisingly the dale itself has over the decades earned the name of Iron Dale and the stones of the workers cottages were probably taken from the ruined abbey in Dale Village. The cottages on Stanhope Street are a good example if you have the time to look at them. Notice the stands of broom screening the first house on the right as you walk by the clubhouse of the Erewash Valley Golf Club.

Eventually you will reach Stanton Hall with its short but traditional gravel drive leading up to the formal entrance. This bygone family seat is now a private nursing home.

Opposite the Chequers is the farm and turning left the narrow walled jitty leading to the gate and stile. Among the farm buildings to your left is an open sided barn. Continue up this track passing directly through dairy and arable farmland to No Mans Lane, a ridge-road beyond the hedgerow on the skyline.

When you top the stile be wary of fast moving traffic. But, when circumstance allows, look at the remains of the tall old oak in the hedgerow. Would you care to put an age to it? Again the photographer can gain a satisfactory study of this tree, especially if there is a good cloud effect in the background.

This is the highest point in the walk and, at 1641 feet, the hills and trees of Charnwood Forest can be seen away to the south, Nottingham's brick and motor mass to the east and the Pennine foothills northwards.

Continue by the tree and over the arable fields and golf course towards Risley Lodge Farm. Bear left of the farm buildings to the stile at the bridleway, which you should cross then climb the stile and go to the footbridge crossing the brook. But do not cross the bridge. Instead turn left alongside the brook and hedgerow.

At the second stile which you need to climb the path curves to the right then swings left uphill and alongside the hedge to the bridlepath. Turn right here down the track and take the path on the left just before you reach the first house.

Cross the fields ahead. Top the stile and you should be alongside the Risley Brook and the adjacent Nature Reserve leased to the Derbyshire Wildlife Trust. The usual plant species listed for this tract of land are adders tongue, fleabane, lady's mantle, and marsh arrow grass. On the margins of the brook you may see the tracks of moorhen, snipe, pied or grey wagtail. A quiet approach may result in a glimpse of one or more of these birds.

To continue, cross the brook and take the path up the hill then down to 'The Nook', the house alongside which you should bear left, then continue by the hawthorn hedge on your left to meet Rushy Lane. Here you need to turn left, cross the road then at the finger post swing right and over three stiles to Stanton road ahead.

After crossing the M1 bridge, continue downhill while taking in the fact that the view of Sandiacre ahead is dominated by the four storey lace factory called Springfield Mills. The tall brick chimney was built by the firm of Terah Hooley Limited in 1888 and lace makers are working there to this day.

On your Sandiacre stretch of road you may glimpse on your right honey fungus attacking the ground ivy that has half covered one of the garden fences.

If you need a snack the local Co-op supermarket is on your right and the Old Village Shop on your left.

Eventually you will see on your left the St Giles play and recreation area. Keep going downhill, taking care at the lane corners and Sandiacre Library car park is only another few hundred yards on.

10. Around Strelley and Cossall

The Route: Moor Farm – Shaws Plantation – Strelley – Cossall – Robinetts Arm – Hemlock Stone

Start: Wollaton Vale Community Centre

How to Get There

By Car: From Derby: A52 to Bramcote Island turning left onto A6002 right onto B6004. Then first (sharp) right at the crossroads passing The Gondola on the right, Wollaton Vale Community Centre a matter of yards along on the right. From Nottingham: A609 to Balloon House crossroads. Turn left and sharp left again onto Wollaton Vale by-passing The Gondola. Community Centre on the right.

By Bus: No.35 from Friar Lane Nottingham alighting at Rosedale Drive. No.25 to terminus from Elite Buildings, Parliament Street. R2 from Derby. Alighting first stop after Bramcote Island (Moor Lane). Walk this lane to North British Housing estate and with railway line on your left to bridge Community Centre on the opposite side.

Distance: 5.5 miles

Duration: 3.5-4 hours. But allow extra 1.5 hours for exploring Oldmoor Wood and the villages of Strelley and Cossall.

Maps: O/S Pathfinder 812 Sheet SK44/54 1:25 000.

The Walk

The motorist who has chosen to park close to the Wollaton Vale Community Centre should proceed up the grass bank, cross Wollaton Vale and walk along the grass verge with his or her back to Nottingham, a housing estate on the right and The Gondola pub on the left.

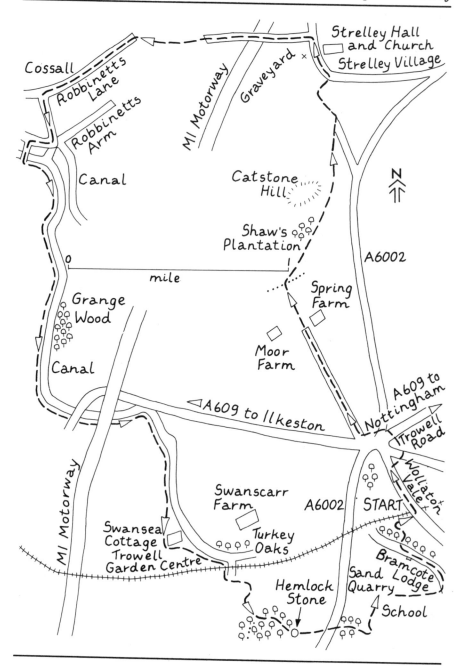

Proceed by Fernwood School and the sad remnants of once sylvan Balloon Woods, then at the traffic lights cross the road to the right (A6009), turn left and cross the A6002 so that the small wood is on your right.

A century ago four turnpike cottages stood here and the road was just wide enough for two carts to pass. When you reach the sign 'Bridleway to Cossall' turn right.

Most of the fields hereabouts are arable but in the past Friesian cattle have been grazed and I recall one evening several cows raising their heads from the grass to watch a vixen threading between their ranks. She passed beneath the farm gate within feet of us, crossed the bridleway then slipped along a path beneath the hedge and across the field on your left. You will see the fox and hare paths threading through the grasses and in May enjoy the scents of the white hawthorn blossom contrasting with the vivid yellows of oilseed rape.

The sizeable tree in the hedgerow on your right is an ash; the smaller trees are oaks. Cow parsley fringes the hedges on either side when you are passing the entrances to Spring Farm. On your right notice the old railway carriages used still, I believe, for storage purposes.

On your left is Moor Farm and once you are past it and the track begins its gradual descent towards the M1 motorway, notice the folds of land screening the sprawls of Trowell and Ilkeston. When you reach the gate by the blue waymarker, turn right through it and up towards Shaws Plantation with the hedge on your right.

Before you and spreading towards the Trent Valley is the city of Nottingham with its prominent high-rise blocks of flats and the occasional gasometer. Never the finest of landscapes but, for contrast, notice the Elizabethan eminence of Wollaton Hall on the sandstone ridge opposite and framed admirably by mature trees. Pink campion flowers along the private farm track to your right and sycamores shade the slopes of Shaws Plantation.

In the winter, particularly, you will see the rabbit warrens (sometimes used by foxes), all·facing east so that you can imagine these animals basking in the early morning light; especially when the ground layer is flourishing from May to July.

Well-walked lane bypassing Strelley Church

As you walk this undulating track, notice the warren entrances along the hedge-bank on your left and from the third field along you may glimpse rabbit families feeding across the unchecked grassy slopes, particularly in the evenings.

Brambles cover the slope to your left but you will no doubt locate several ramblers' paths dividing the ground cover and thickets and leading to the hollow where several insignificant stones have given the slope its name 'Catstone Hill'. But why? I see little in the shapes of either one of these grey abutments that even faintly resembles a member of the feline species.

A few local folk have reminded me that the stones and hollow are connected with the Druids, therefore the cats may have been used for sacrificial purposes. Catstone Hill is today used for motorbike scrambling and no more scenic than the litter dumped usually by the gate that takes you onto the sand track which is not sharp left; but second left between the hedgerows with the beech trees to your left.

As you are walking, the red bricked and pantile roofed cottages of Strelley village can be glimpsed between the trees over to your right and notice that solitary tree in the middle of the field; memorable that, in shape and size.

Where the land bends you will see Strelley church, the Hall and its surrounding cedars across the paddock. If you lean on this fence on a summer morning at first light, there is a chance you may see a barn owl hunting across the fields and over the underground reservoir.

The lane meets with the road bend and if you choose to go right there are some interesting cottages to be seen and a delightful hostelry, 'The Broad Oak'. After visiting these then you need to return to this point to continue the walk. A section on Strelley village you will find a few pages on.

Lodgegate Cottage, Strelley Hall – notice the 'buttress' style of building

Turning left towards the church you will, I hope, experience the rural atmosphere while admiring the structure of the twelfth century tower ahead and the cedars in the walled grounds to your right.

After exploring the church notice the sturdy cottages built with exterior buttresses and recesses. Strelley Hall has since been converted into offices housing a local firm.

A matter of yards from the green 'footpath' sign on your left is a white tubular gate with the sign 'Private Road Old Moor Farmhouse and Turkey Fields Farm' fastened to it. Go through the gap and between the trees on your left is a fine pastoral scene for the photographer to consider. Though trimmed, the hedgerow nurtures a host of wild plants and flowers including some interesting stands of meadow cranesbill, those pale blue five petalled flowers that grow in clumps along both sides of the path.

Once you have crossed the M1 motorway bridge, there is Oldmoor Pool in the vale on the left and a comparatively new track for the Notts Anglers to proceed downfield to the water, while one of the several signs informs us that it is not a footpath. Oldmoor Wood stretches away from the pool. Now owned by the Woodland Trust, there's a sign at their field entrance 'Visitors Are Welcome To Walk In This Wood'.

How different from the anglers' sign you have just passed! And believe me Oldmoor is an ancient and interesting wood, so if you have the time, why not divert for half an hour or so.

Those trees in the long belt to your right are mainly oak and sycamore. At the horse field on the left pause to look at the red-bricked farmhouse and few outbuildings tucked among the trees, but overlooked by that solitary Scots pine.

When you reach three forks, continue along the narrow central lane ahead. There is what appears to be a private coal mining concern over to your right. Notice the old brambly hedge highlighted by the pink fires of rosebay willow herb in midsummer, ablaze with berries throughout the autumn. There are some fine oaks and where the track dips an evergreen or 'holme' oak supporting a stand of holly.

At the lane's end there is a willow clump to the right and another 'holme' oak to your left. Turn left and ease through the gap beside the rusted tubular gate and walk the lane beside the mixed hedgerows. As you are walking, notice the unchecked grasses in the fields to your right and the sprawl of Ilkeston, the third largest town in Derbyshire, beyond.

The grey house 'Moss Cottage' on your left was probably once a farmhouse. Turn right with the lane, noticing more unchecked thicket and scrubland to your left; wild flower and wildlife havens such places as these.

Another five minutes walking takes you alongside the houses on the eastern edge of Cossall village, by-passing Grange Farm on the right. Literary-minded walkers will be aware that Cossall was the home of Louise Burrows, fiancee of D H Lawrence. The cottage where this attractive lady lived with her parents is situated next but one to the church, as I will remind you in the 'brief histories' section relating to the villages of Strelley and Cossall.

The downhill road with the slightly leaning oak tree on the left will take you to another interesting place; it is to this junction that you need to return, if you have chosen to look around Cossall church.

You should be walking on the right facing oncoming traffic, and carefully. After a few hundred yards you will notice the remains of the Nottingham canal over the hedge on your right. But still with oncoming traffic in mind you should be looking for the gate opposite and where a length of the canal crosses beneath the road. By way of another diversion, go through the gate and just stroll along the bank here. It is a lovely spot this; frequented by moorhens and water-voles. Small birds and wood pigeons come to the waterside to drink. In midsummer, yellow water-lilies make an eyecatching study and a few weeks later you can watch the dragonflies hunting for insects around and between the stalks of reed and common sedge.

This narrow and welcoming stretch of water is known as Robbinettes Arm and was used as a route for singular barges connecting with a private railway and of course the transportation of stone, coal and pit props. Today the outlet feeds the pool situated between the motorway and Oldmoor Wood.

Watch for the traffic when leaving Robbinettes by the same gate and go through the opposite gate with the canal on your left.

A change of scene here, reeds, willows, moorhens, coots and a pair of mute swans. Walk to the footbridge and cross it turning left so that the canal is on your left. This divided arm of the waterway was known to the canal linesmen as Cossall Forks.

Follow the canal right down to the car park, which is situated on the original canal bed, then go through the gate and proceed along the official Canal Trail, which I am sorry to say is now a comparatively dry walk. However there are several small pools along the way and eventually you will pass Grange Wood, once so inaccessible that foxes used regularly to breed there.

The past always catches up with one here for I have known the waterway for thirty or forty years, but space does not allow for my lamentations and for this fact I am sure you will be grateful. Beyond the main road bridge and the reeds you can see the feeders and overflows. Ahead is the M1 motorway with its volumes of traffic heavy now even through the night.

Where the waterway ends, turn left onto the main road and pass beneath the M1, then go up the embankment on your right and take up with the towpath so that the dry canal bed is on your left. In one of those lovely roadside cottages incidentally lived the last canal linesman, Mr Thornhill, who gave up his 'steady' job at Stanton for an outdoor occupation.

On the bend and across the far side is Trowell Basin where once barges were loaded and off loaded with coal, stone and agricultural products. In later years it served as a nesting site for a pair of mute swans. Coot and moorhen families also ferried through the reeds.

Ahead is the beautifully arched Swansea Bridge, built from local stone and partially covered with ivy. In the hedgerow to your right is a stile alongside a young oak. Climb the stile and follow the hedgerow on the left, glimpsing (and hearing) the motorway in the vale to your right there.

The buildings beyond the hedge are part of the now much extended Trowell Garden Centre which has been converted from the canal foreman's home originally called Swansea Cottage. Today it is a thriving industry, but I can remember cycling by the whitewashed cottage on hot sunny days when the waterside lawn played host to a family of swans and cygnets that used to preen and sleep there.

You can wander the spacious centre which sells a vast selection of products. There is a small but adequate coffee bar if you are in need of refreshment and lectures on gardening and flower arranging take place on certain weekends according to the season.

While you are looking around the buildings you will meet again with the canal bed which is dry but still discernible as it bends between those sandstone ledges. On a section of the disused towpath stands the grinding stone on which the canal linesmen used to sharpen their scythes.

Returning to the main entrance – or continuing the walk, turn left with the garden centre fence on your left and follow the slip path round onto the canal towpath.

You should now be walking with your back to the garden centre. A profusion of small wild birds can usually be seen throughout the thickets and hedgerows. Notice the fox and badger paths cutting darkly through the dry reeds.

On the tight bend among the hedgerow thickets are two splendid turkey oaks. On the higher slope, Swanscarr Farm, derelict at the time of writing, but scheduled to become a clubhouse for the long-envisaged golf course that has yet to be laid across the fields (July 1992).

Swanscarr Farm was built in the 1780s and its name probably derives from the flooded willow and alder thickets or 'carr' where swans and wildfowl once fed, but in which the water has long since been diverted to form the main channel of the canal.

But what you are looking for now on the right is the hedgegap and path that will take you over the railway bridge. Follow the path to the steep steps and, after your careful descent, turn left, climb the stile and follow the path around the right-hand side of the field to the steep slopes that

These distinctively-shaped Turkey oaks are on the slope between Swanscarr Farm and the dry bed of the Nottingham Canal

lead you up through Stapleford Hill Wood. Here, in May, bluebells enhance the glades and the cuckoo still calls from the oaks and sycamores.

Eventually you will see a housing estate down-slope to your right and small caves in the sandstone abutment. Just continue between the trees until you can pick out the not so definable path over to your left, then cross to it and a few paces on you will find yourself looking at the Hemlock Stone.

Some sad graffiti on it this side I am afraid, so make your way between the scrub-oak to its far side. Notice the texture of the sandstone and for a brief account turn a few pages on. Turning from this roadside landmark, walk over the crossing to the stile situated alongside the estate offices of the Broxtowe Borough Council – once a gamekeeper's cottage and outbuildings.

Close-up of the sandstone texture forming the bulk structure of the Hemlock Stone at Bramcote

Walk now along the perimeter fence with the quarries down on your left and Bramcote Woods to your right. If you keep on along the fence you will reach a recess and a gap with a footpath sign alongside. Pass through this and walk with the college campus to your right. At the next stile turn right and after a few strides you will be passing Moor Farm which in recent years has become a restaurant with public bars and a change of name to Bramcote Manor.

When this narrow lane meets with Moor Lane you need to turn left, but the Derby walker would do better to turn right and walk down the lane at the bottom of which is the main Nottingham-Derby road. (Derby is to your right). By crossing to the far side you can catch an R2 or almost any bus to Derby.

Nottingham folk should continue down Moor Lane, once known as Brickyard Lane and one of the longest established routes in the area, to the wooded banks.

You need to be looking for the built in steps to the right. Make you way down these (sorry about the litter) and into one of the walkways threading between the North British Housing estate. Take a left turn and walk along Fylingdale Way with the railway line on your left to the bridge, which you need to cross and close to which your car will (hopefully) be waiting.

Bus passengers have a choice: either the 25 with the stop on the grass bank by the community centre (but note there is no such bus on Sunday) or the 35 which you can catch by standing at the shelter on the opposite side of Wollaton Vale (and twice every hour on Sunday).

Brief Histories of Strelley and Cossall

Strelley

Situated within five miles of Nottingham's busy city centre, Strelley is a squirearchal village with its original cottages built for the employees of the Strelley Hall estate, set back along both sides of the main road. Were it not for the understandable and growing popularity of its single pub 'The Broad Oak', it would still have retained the solitude of a bygone age. The squires of Strelley were represented first by the Strelley family, whose succession extended from Norman times until 1678 when the estate was purchased by Ralph Edge, who on three occasions was elected Lord Mayor Nottingham. The Hall is a house of Georgian design which, since the death of the last Edge descendant, has been taken over but left unspoilt by a local firm. Of the church Pevsner wrote that it was 'without doubt the most important church on the western outskirts of Nottingham'. Built by Sir Sampson De Strelley around 1356, the ancestral tombs are inside an ornate chancel. The nearby nave was similarly described as 'the finest rood screen in Nottinghamshire'. The finest and most fitting monument is considered that awarded to Sir Sampson, the church founder.

Cossall

Farmhouses, holdings and cottages stand alongside two sharply angled road bends, but it is not until the church spire comes into view that one associates this village with D H Lawrence, who was engaged to Louise Burrows. Her father, Alfred, lived with his wife and family at Church

Cottage and displayed his talent for carving the recedos in the nearby church. Lawrence described Cossall church as 'the old little church with its small spire on a square tower'. Behind are the remains of a long dried-up moat. In Lawrence's fine novel 'The Rainbow', Cossall is disguised as Cossetthay and William Brangwen was, in fact, Alfred Burrows. Ursula, his daughter, was Lawrence's fiancee Louise and judging by the few prints displayed in the Lawrence autobiographies, she was a photogenic and darkly attractive young lady. A modern bungalow stands on the site of Marsh Farm where Lawrence told us 'the Brangwens had lived for generations'. He also described the house standing 'in the meadows where the Erewash twisted sluggishly through alder trees separating Derbyshire from Nottinghamshire'.

Bell Pits and a Waggonway

In the fields around Strelley traces of the bell pits are still discernible – at least to those interested in industrial archaeology. Owned by Percival Willoughby of Wollaton, these pits were leased by Huntingdon Beaumont, whose family home was in Leicestershire. It has been locally well endorsed that these pits were producing 20,000 tons of coal a year at the beginning of the seventeenth century. This amount apparently was said to be half the total coal output for the entire country at the time! Huntingdon Beaumont also originated a wooden waggonway along which coal was hauled from the bell pit fields southwards to Wollaton Road and from there on to Nottingham. The waggonway was probably laid in the early sixteenth century.

The Hemlock Stone

The prominence of Bunter Sandstone has for long been the instigator of stories about Druid associations within the area, but the realists, myself included, are extremely doubtful. Surrounded by green slopes and wooded glades, it has certainly been a trysting place for lovers and a picnic spot for couples and families, while in his novel 'Sons and Lovers' Lawrence ventured: 'They had expected a venerable and dignified monument. They found a little, gnarled, twisted stump of rock, something like a decayed mushroom standing out pathetically on the side of a field.' About the height of the Hemlock Stone I intend to say little, since one source of information gives thirty feet and another sixty-seven. Nor do I intend to climb it with a tape measure as my companion, although the graffiti gangs have been up with their aerosol sprays, as you will have noticed. Of its origin, however, I accept the theories of several other local wanderers, who believe it to be part of a sandstone cliff which has completely eroded, leaving this single spur within its sand grains protected by a layer of barium sulphate.

Moor Farm

Moor Farm is believed to have been a medieval holding and certainly the land below the sandstone ridge appears to have been good for animals and arable. If you sit outside the pub and restaurant with a pint of bitter before you on a warm summer evening, you can trace the farmhouse apart from its extensions and, if I were with you, I'd undoubtedly mention the recreation field extending from the horse paddocks to what is now The Canal Trail, for that tract of land was used for grazing Lincolnshire Red Polled cattle when I first walked the footpath with my father in the Nineteen Forties.

The Moor Farm Ghosts

Way back in those boyhood days I was told that Moor Farm was haunted by the spirit of a girl who lost her legs in an accident. Past families had said they heard sounds resembling someone crawling along a corridor. So unhappy was this young lady that she used a length of rope and a beam, in what is now the pool room, to take her own life. Some claim that they can occasionally feel her brooding presence lingering in that room. Other sounds are those that can only be associated with a boy or girl bouncing a ball. However one lady, who was visiting the hostelry for the first time, saw the apparition of a priest rounding a corner again near the pool room. There are several other records of a priest being glimpsed and in comparatively recent times.

Moor Lane

Moor Lane runs alongside Moor Farm and connects Coventry Lane to the main Nottingham-Derby Road. It is one of the oldest trackways in the region and was established long before Blackbird Lane was renamed Coventry Lane and widened to ease the traffic flow between Stapleford and Bilborough. Originally known as Brickyard Lane, the still narrow walkway was laid with clay, cobbles and bricks over which horses pulled carts to the brickyard situated near Ballooon Woods. The bricks were bought by the ton for the Nottingham building contractors, but the problem was, that unlike today, the lane swept up the steep sides of Bramcote Hill and the horse teams pulling a cartload of bricks experienced hardship to the extent of a cart occasionally overturning. However, negotiations with the owners of Moor Farm resulted in extra horses being grazed and stabled there. These in turn were harnessed to the existing team. In this way enough horsepower enabled each cart to be pulled up the hill. Today no such hill brow exists because dynamite was used to cut a satisfactory route through the terrain. Derby walkers, turning down Moor Lane to catch the homeward bus, might find the initials and dates carved into the sandstone either side of the lane interesting, although 1924 seems to have been the earliest that someone decided to cut their initials.

11. A Family Exploration of Wollaton Park, Nottingham

The Route: Car park – Digby Avenue – Moatside Path – Arbour Hill – Lakeside – Courtyards – Formal Gardens

Start: The car park nearest the Barn Restaurant. But Derby walkers arriving by bus, see footnote.

How to Get There

By Car: From Nottingham, the route is along the A609 and is well signposted. From Derby along A52 to Bramcote Island. Go around this then turn second left into Thoresby Road; Over next island and into Wollaton Village, turning right at Admiral Rodney T-junction; down the hill to second set of lodge gates on the right.

By Bus: From Nottingham No.25 from Elite Buildings, Parliament Street, Nottingham to Lodge One Gates. But no such bus on Sunday. An alternative is No.35 from Friar Lane. From Derby R2 to Beeston Lodge Gates on Derby Road.

Distance: 3.5 – 4 miles approximately

Duration: 2.5 hours but longer to allow for stops etc. Ideal for half day exploration.

Maps: Not essential as route chosen for basic interest in a bygone country estate. But Estates Red Book if map is needed.

Footnote: This explorative walk has been divided into two parts so that one can join it from the nearest entrance. Derby walkers arriving on R2 can begin at Route Two and work through the walk to Route One, returning to their original route and the homeward bus.

The Walk: Route One

The singular tree alongside these car park oaks is a Wellingtonia Pine. Embracing some 524 acres of enclosed land Wollaton Park once nurtured over 135 different tree species.

To begin the walk, look towards the children's playground and the Barn Restaurant. The barn was, until recent times, part of the working farm, the entrance of which was established between Lodge One and the barn's north entrance. The derelict farmhouse is hidden from sight.

Walk towards the children's playground and turn with it on your left, then proceed along by the wall noting the height and width of the beech trees. Pause at the high wrought iron gates in the wall to your left and peer into the kitchen gardens. Those dividing walls are hollow and along certain sections a 'bothie' containing a cooking range and bed space was established. This enabled the gardeners of bygone times to work a night shift by keeping fires lit within the hollow walls, for the exteriors were hung with apricots, peaches and nectarines.

The Head Gardener's house, still habitable, is in a quiet corner and screened by mature lime, beech and yew trees. Walk now to the belt of rough grass, Lombardy poplar and silver birch trees, then turn with it on your left. These trees were planted in 1928 to act as a windbreak for the crops which were grown on this long tract of land known today as 'the rugby pitches' but originally called Goodes Field.

It is worth mentioning that during the last war flax was grown here, for surprisingly, the stalks of this crop were used in the manufacture of parachute ropes and supports.

Where the tree belt joins the fenced plantation, known as Gorsebed Wood, you may see a trickle of spring water gleaming among the osiers. It is here that the red deer stags, which roam the parklands at will, open up their 'wallows' in late August or early September, a few weeks preceding the autumn's rut. In the long grass you will also see the trails made by fox and badger.

Walk now with that tract of open woodland to your right and the fenced plantation to your left. If you are walking quietly in the early morning

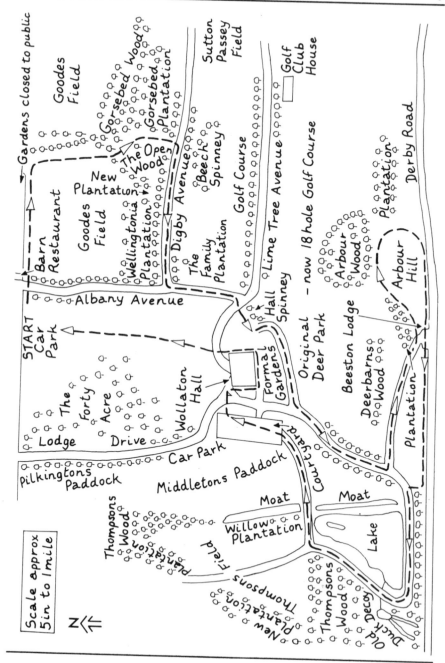

here you may well see a fox or litter of fox cubs exploring the glades.

The trees incidentally have been planted to replace the old trees that the inter gales are beginning to bring down. Among them are quite a number of American Red Oak and splendid they look in late October or early November.

When you reach the fence corner, pause at the deer entrance gap and notice the rhododendron thickets and pines in Gorsebed Wood. This was once a pheasant covert maintained by a gamekeeper and wherever you see rhododendron planted in this way it is a sign that pheasants were the main game crop, intended to provide sport for the shooting gentry in the autumn and winter months.

Walk now upslope with a fenced plantation to your left and the open woods to your right. A few strides and you are on a green ride known as Digby Avenue. A gamekeeper's lodge was once situated at the end of this ride, but the site has long since given way to a road (Eton Grove) of detached houses.

Turn right noticing the still flourishing oaks and few dead walnut trees with the golf course and open beech spinney to your left. Again in the autumn this is the best place to watch the red and fallow deer feeding on the harvests of acorns and beech mast. But a word of warning. Do not attempt to touch a red deer stag.

Tawny owls can be heard fluting here on frosted nights and grey squirrels have long since replaced the red. As you are nearing the top of the avenue note two more plantations, one of which is on the golf course. This is The Family Plantation with the oaks and rhododendrons having been planted by the Middleton family to provide food and shelter for the deer. The eighteen hole golf course here was in 1926-29 laid across the original Deer Park.

To your right is a new plantation, again with trees intended to replace those nearing their dotage, and a rounded wood of Wellingtonia pines which would have reached greater proportions had they not been planted on a layer of Bunter Sandstone.

Wollaton Hall and the formal gardens are situated on the crest of the slope before you, but you the walker needs to bear slightly left and up the gentle slope with the oak spinney over on the left and the dry moat partially encircling the formal gardens on the right. Among those oaks are the greenkeepers' sheds and, as you are making for the moatside path or narrow track that runs between the golf course and the dry moat, see the avenue of limes coming on your left.

Needing a formal coaching drive and visualising it extending from the formal park entrance to the front steps of his country seat, many landowners took the advice of John Evelyn who, in his book 'Silva' published in the sixteenth century, said that besides being members of the tea-bush family, limes were fast growing trees suitable for a country house environment; thus the popularity of this species became established. A second 'vogue' in tree planting occurred in later years and this I shall mention farther along on the walk.

Wollaton's formal entrance incidentally is on the main Nottingham-Derby Road separated by an estate of houses and bungalows built on 300 acres of the original Wollaton Park.

Walking now along the moatside path the broad sweep of golf course is known as Arbour Hill. Notice the copper beeches here; over to your right are the summer house and cedar lawns where crinoline ladies once strolled. Many of the periphery cedars have been felled in recent gales.

Arbour Hill is the main breeding territory of the red deer hinds. Consequently from July the spotted calves can be seen following a hind or family group. When you reach the end of the moatside path pause to take in the peaceful scene of the lake in the wooded hollow.

To the right of the lake is Thompson Paddock; on either side and partially surrounding the lake is Thompsons Wood, named after the woodsman responsible for planting the original trees. But only in the last twenty years has the willow plantation on the right been planted along with the two plantations screening the houses overlooking the park.

Turn now with the golf course on your left and the lime avenue on your right. The wood on the golf course to your left is Deerbarns Wood, so called because in Middleton times a three sided barn attracted the deer which in the winter gathered here to feed on the swedes and mangolds brought daily by the estate workmen.

At the bottom of the hill there is a diversion. You can either take the path around the lake or have a look around Arbour Hill, but returning to the lakeside in due course.

Assuming you have chosen Arbour Hill, then continue along the path noticing the bracken and trees to your right. Eventually you will see Beeston Lodge gates on your right but keep along by the fence of yet another plantation with the fox and badger trails threading through the undergrowth.

Turn with the plantation still on your left and take the steep path up to the wood of rhododendron and pine. Turn right and pause to take in the splendour of the hilltop oak. Notice the breadth of its trunk or bole, and try to imagine some bygone gentleman or estate worker taking his ease up here and looking at the neighbouring estate of Highfields (now the Nottingham University campus) and the Trent valley flood-plain beyond.

Was the oak planted here intentionally, do you think? Beyond the next plantation is a length of practise golf course and the club house situated alongside the lime avenue. But you need again to have the plantation on your left then turn with the main Nottingham-Derby Road below the fringe of oaks, limes and rhododendron thicket.

The Walk: Part Two

The turreted gatehouse of Beeston Lodge is worth studying for it was built as a secondary formal gateway an also to house two of the estate's working families, probably in the mid to late eighteenth century. Two small gardens extended along the side of the wall and free range poultry were still being fed from the lodge on the right in the early Sixties.

However the lodge gates are now derelict but beyond the locked entrance doors a stone spiral staircase leads to the small kitchen, bedroom, bathroom and sitting room. Nor did the inhabitants hear the traffic in the way one would were they living here today, for I have an old postcard showing cattle being driven along the main Nottingham-Derby Road with not a gig or charabanc in sight.

In those bygone times the lodge gates were kept locked and anyone wanting to enter the park needed to ring a bell; one of the gatekeeper's wives answered, often by calling from a trapdoor, traces of which can be seen if you stand within the arch and look up. Should the caller not have been expected, there was every chance that they were turned away.

On now with the parks boundary wall to your left and bordered by lime trees, which again look magnificent on a sunlit day in mid October. In the bracken are lime, yew, holly and London plane trees.

When you reach the wood, turn with the chestnut paling to your left. If you are strolling alone here early in the morning there is a good chance of seeing a fox hunting along the wooded slopes and grey squirrels are a foregone conclusion. The path takes you down to the lake path, but before turning left, notice the original bank of the lake in this rounded expanse of shallows.

Designed from a tract of marshland in the eighteenth century, the water level reached the side of the path until the early nineteen Sixties when colliery subsidence caused cracks to appear in the base and a considerable amount of water was lost. The lake bed also tilted slightly thus leaving the few yards of walkable sand along the edge such as we see today.

Besides coot, moorhen and mallard, the reed bed shelters great-crested grebe, reed bunting and reed warbler. The current mute swan pair have been at Wollaton for ten years and nest alongside the length of chestnut fencing which has been erected to protect them from vandals; a prolific breeding pair there are some years when they hatch nine or ten cygnets from a clutch of eleven eggs.

By turning left along the path you will again see some quite splendid beech trees. Where the path turns right what appears to be a waterless bridge is the original Middleton boat-house where two rowing boats were moored and the servant staff were rowed out by the Hall's valet on Wednesday afternoons.

Down in the tract of woodland to your left you will notice two or three long drainage channels and on slightly higher ground among the rhododendron thickets a reeded pool; known locally as 'The Swamps'.

These are the remnants of the Middleton's main duck decoy. As you draw level with the pool you may glimpse a stand of yew trees. Wherever you see these planted in the centre of a wood it is safe to assume that they once screened a keepers shooting hut, where a change of clothes and the inevitable bottle of whisky were stored! The wide stretch of water to your right is known as The Dam. The sides are now concrete, but the banks have seen better times with a length of chestnut fencing separating the anglers from the strolling public and alder trees attracting kingfishers. I was talking here with an angler when a kingfisher flew in and perched on his rod. I have also watched a nuthatch flying down from the tee branches and seizing some squirming maggots from the angler's tin.

The woodland glades are photogenic but again originally intended to provide cover for the many pheasants that were bred here.

The island in the north arm of the lake attracts the red deer stags into the water to feed on the strands of willow. Both stags and hinds can also be seen stripping the sedges and chewing strands of Canadian pondweed. Where you reach the end of the woodland path, the route swings right, takes you over the moat bridge and up towards the court yards and Hall. But for a longer walk you can go through the gate on your left and follow the woods edge fence around Thompsons Paddock, or after the gate follow the path to your right that runs beside the willow wood. Both routes take you to the end of the dry moat and you can then cross Middleton's Paddock with red, fallow deer and white park cattle grazing and a cricket field separating this paddock from Pilkington's Paddock which slopes up to the park's boundary wall. Another word of warning: keep to the higher ground for the lower tracts are likely to be marshy.

For the basic walk then, turn right and walk up the path towards the Hall. Eventually you will be walking in line with the courtyards to the left and I have added a few historical notes on these a few pages on. But from this point you are in an ideal situation to be exploring them. After doing so, however, return to the clock here then walk up the narrow paved path to the tunnel entrance of the formal gardens.

When you are at the diversion of paths notice the rockery and heather garden on your right and the camelia house to the left. Wander through this vinery and at its south end is a notice explaining is function. The same can be said for the rose garden.

Walk now with the cedar lawn on your right to the steps which will take you up to the south lawns terrace and goldfish pond. This south entrance was much used by the Hall's bygone residents and below the terrace steps is the original bowling alley. When you are standing with Wollaton Hall before you turn right and follow the path around to your right. Ahead you will see the gates, either side of which are two magnificent evergreen or (Holme) oaks.

To visit the Hall turn left for the formal (north) entrance, or keep straight on down the hill and across the wide Forty Acre field to the car park. There are Blue Atlas Cedar trees on the slope to your right. As you are walking, I will finally explain that the Forty Acre field has served several functions, having been rented out as grazing land to tenant farmers before being enclosed as a camp for German and Italian prisoners during the last war. Today the field is regarded as Wollaton Park's showground for summer tenting events including the Autocarna and the Nottingham City Show.

The car park is ahead. Derby walkers should turn right and cross to the children's playground, thus picking up the Route One from there.

The Wollaton Deer Rut

When the first acorns litter the ground beneath the oaks, both the red and fallow deer search for and feed voraciously upon them as if addicted to the rich calcium they contain.

This time of year, the onset of autumn coincides with the beginning of the mating season or 'rut', when the red deer stags regard other members of the hierarchy as rivals and the same can be said for the mature fallow bucks.

For some unknown reason the lowering temperatures increase the activities of both stag and buck, the former wallowing around the edge of the lake or moat, the latter digging 'scrapes' with his forehooves and rolling over it after he has injected urine and semen over the spot. Thus the walker can occasionally catch the 'rutty' scent of a fallow buck or stag.

The large dominant stags each parade around and attempt to gain the interest of a group of hinds as do the fallow bucks the does. The stags' resonant roars carry for some distance on a frosted day, while one needs to be walking alongside Thompsons Wood to hear the deep, gutteral grunts emitted by the fallow buck.

Red deer stags use two types of roar: one intended to call in more hinds, the other to warn rivals to stay clear of his territory. Antler interlocked battles occur between rival stags and rival bucks and once I watched two stags interlocked for a full twenty-two minutes before they withdrew. Occasionally a combatant is savagely gored and fatalities are not unknown, in fact most deer parks lose at least one fallow buck due to it having been fatally gored in a rutting battle.

September: young Red Deer stags, with Wollaton Hall in the background

Both the red deer hinds and the fallow does cross the parklands according to wind direction and the need to feed upon acorns and beech mast. The dominant stags or bucks move with them.

A hind or doe comes into 'oestrus' for twenty-four hours every third week during September or October, but is usually covered by a male of the respective species during the first bout of heat.

Neither the stags nor bucks feed for six weeks and, as the autumn increases and more hinds and does are covered, the rivalry between males increases as the number of females yet to come into 'oestrus' become fewer.

The rut of both the red and fallow-deer reaches its peak throughout the third week in October. For the walker, observer or photographer this can prove to be a very interesting time, but as one who has studied and worked with deer, I advise the interested observer to remain within thirty or forty feet of a rutting stag, while studying the behaviour patterns aided by binoculars. There is no need to fear these animals but caution should be exercised both among children and adults, for the occasional stag has been known to have attacked unwary or over confident members of the public.

The Willoughbys of Wollaton

The first person of note in the history of Wollaton was Ralph Bugge, a wealthy trader in wools and woads who acquired an estate at Willoughby on the Wolds around 1280. His surname was eventually dropped and enhanced by the grand title of his grandson 'Sir Richard de Willoughby'. Ralph's son was also called Richard and he married Isabella, heiress to the fortunes of the de Mortens, a family of landowners already established at Wollaton.

Ralph and his relatives had built the first Wollaton Hall which was situated close to the church and rectory. The stones from this building are believed to have been those one sees today in the main structure of the low walls on either side of Church Hill, which links Wollaton Road with the village.

The hilltop site of the second Wollaton Hall was selected by Francis Willoughby (1546-96) for he had found wealth from the coal mined throughout the manorial pits.

Critics of Willoughby called Wollaton Hall an expensive luxury. The formal entrance faces north, but the residents apparently made much use of the south terrace. Engraved in a couplet on the south side of the building are the words 'Behold this house of Francis Willoughby, Knight. With rare art built, to Willoughbys bequeathed. Begun 1580 and finished 1588'. This latter date was also the year of the Spanish Armada.

Ancestor stone was used for the basic structure of the Hall and this was exchanged for coal extracted from the Wollaton pits. The expense of building and furnishing such a magnificent house and the provision of dowries for his three daughters left Sir Francis in permanent debt and estranged from his family. He died alone, in London, in 1596.

Other noticeable members of the family were the explorer Sir Hugh Willoughby who in 1554 died in the Arctic, while attempting to discover a north easterly route between Cathay and India, and Francis Willoughby (1635-72) the famous naturalist and friend of John Ray.

Through various descendants the family name changed to Middleton and, following the close death of His Lordship and Ladyship, the entire estate was auctioned off. On the 18 May 1925 the Hall and Park were purchased by the Corporation of Nottingham for the sum of £200,000, but to recoup this the Corporation sold 274 acres to property developers, leaving the Hall and 524 acres for the people of Nottingham to enjoy.

12. Exploring Long Eaton

The Route: Erewash Canal – Long Eaton – Cranfleet Canal – Trent Lock – Erewash Canal

Start: Bridge Street Car Park, Sandiacre

How to Get There

By Car: From Derby – to Risley (B5010). Over traffic lights at canal bridge Sandiacre then turning left for car park. From Nottingham – Along Derby Road and through Stapleford. Just before the canal bridge at Sandiacre turn right (Bridge Street) into car park.

By Bus: Regular service from Nottingham and Derby to Sandiacre

Distance: 5 miles approximately

Duration: 3 – 3.5 hours

Maps: O/S Land Ranger 129 1:50 000 or Pathfinder 833 SK43/53) 1:25 000

The Walk

From Bridge Street car park take the short pedestrian walkway to the towpath of the Erewash Canal and pause to look at the tall chimney of Springfield Mill which was built in 1888 specifically for the production of lace.

Fifteen to twenty mute swans gather around the bridge and preen on the opposite grass bank around December and January when the shrubs and posts are strung with the colourful baubles of Christmas lights.

Turn now with your back to the mill and follow the towpath under the bridge and along to the great concrete supports of the bridge that takes the Stapleford By-pass (A52) over the water.

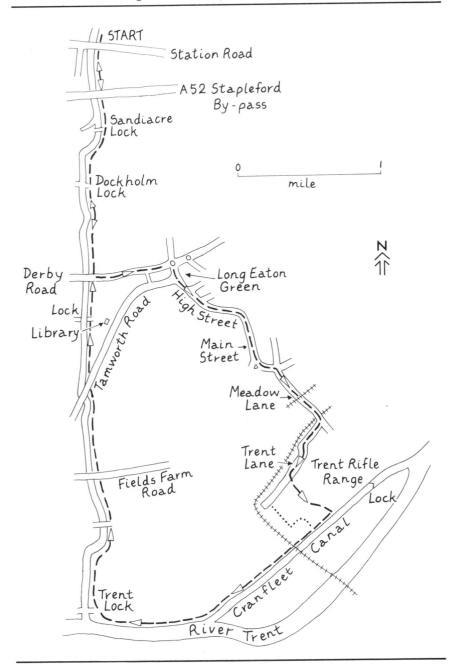

Twenty years ago, I called at one of the houses on the other side of the canal and was told by its lady occupant that in years gone by the area was so rural kingfishers used to perch on the front garden gate!

However, once you are heading towards Sandiacre Lock the roar of traffic seems already to be subsiding. At the small weir look left beyond the hedgerows and glimpse the reeds and water of The Ballast Hole which is now an anglers resort and fed to some extent by water from the Erewash canal. Where the canal bends to the right you will see beyond the hump backed bridge a lock-gate which once connected the barges with the now forgotten Derby Canal. The cottage at Sandiacre Lock is one of those I have always wished I'd lived in, except that it is reputedly haunted, although by whom or what I haven't yet discovered.

Sandiacre Lock

Beyond Sandiacre Lock the canal bends then straightens alongside the houses where ducks paddle and longboats are moored beside a splendid willow. I was once shown a wartime photograph of a swan pair escorting an unusually large brood of fourteen cygnets along the stretch of the canal and so the aquatic weed on which these birds feed would have been as equally prolific then.

Across the fields to your left are the Toton Railway sidings; Toton hereabouts being pronounced Toeton as I expect you are already aware. This was once recognised as one of the largest railway marshalling yards in Europe and although its situation has over the past two decades shown a marked decline, it is now regarded as one of the largest diesel maintenance depots in the country.

Continue down the towpath beyond Dockholm Lock and bridge noticing how the householders have merged their gardens into the canal-side scene by planting willow trees and positioning garden seats. On the bends notice the reeds growing thickly alongside the mill and factory walls. Moorhens and coots use these as nesting sites.

When you reach the bridge spanning Derby Road, Long Eaton, go beneath it, then take those steps to your left up onto the road. From here you can either turn right and proceed along the people-thronged road into the town centre or left across the bridge to have a look at the mills to which I have referred in a further section. If you do this you will need to cross the bridge again to continue the walk.

The main council offices are in these pleasant grounds across the road to the left. When you reach the traffic island, known locally as Long Eaton Green, just keep along the pavement into the old Market Place. Use the pelican crossing and turn right along the opposite pavement so that you have Long Eaton Green at your back.

The precinct area where you crossed was once the market place long established and nurturing a strong social atmosphere. Not that the atmosphere has been totally lost due to the current spread of market stalls, but the precinct really came into its own at Christmas-time when it's admirably bedecked with lights.

Turn with the street corners so that you are passing the main Cooperative shop with The Royal Hotel almost opposite. At the traffic lights, cross and walk along Main Street to the island at the end, then cross again and turn right into Meadow Lane. Check that you have the railway bridge ahead and after this cross at the gates then make a sharp right turn into Trent Lane.

The embankment is on your right; eventually those houses on the left will give way to a firing range. Fields come into view and the wooded banks of the River Trent. Well clear of the targets, Friesian cattle are usually grazing the field you have to cross and beyond the gate or stile is a tussocky farm track which, if you follow it to the right, will take you to a stile and the towpath of the Cranfleet canal.

Turn right and follow the towpath to where the canal joins the Trent. Boating, angling and a pub, 'The Trent Navigation' are the main attractions of this much visited resort known locally as Trent Lock.

Winter moorings on the Erewash Canal at Trent Lock, with the Radcliffe-on-Soar cooling towers beyond

You can use The Trent Navigation as your pointer if you are going to look around, but to continue the walk you need the river at your back. Notice as you are lingering by the lock the cooling towers of Radcliffe on Soar power station and find the notes relating to this site a few pages on.

The lock keeper at the cottage near The Trent Navigation is a genial man, who understandably enjoys a conversation revolving around the river, its traffic and wildlife. Those are his free-range hens, cockerel and goat in the nearby orchard.

To continue the walk, have the Erewash canal to your left, hedgerow on the right. Notice the differing shapes and sizes of the houseboats and moored craft. One houseboat owner with whom I've recently spoken bemoaned the fact that all the pleasure seems to be going out of boating. By that, I mean when you are queuing up to go through the gates each summer weekend, it feels as if half the British population is out on the river.

Near the railway bridge, notice the marina to your right; more colourful by far than when it was standing derelict between the end of the war and the Seventies. When you reach the Tamworth Road bridge, those are stands of reeds, sedge and willow fringing the opposite bank. Mallard, moorhens, coot and a pair of mute swans nest here. Reed buntings and pied wagtails use the reeds as cover; nor has the boating traffic depleted the beds of yellow water-lily.

Where the low wall ends on your right, a gap takes you onto the pavement, but this is only by way of a diversion, because your main route is along the towpath. However, if you are interested in visiting a local artists or photography exhibition, follow the pavement along to the left by the Fire Station and you will reach the library, surrounded by a garden and with an old-fashioned exterior, but refurbished and well organised within.

I cannot guarantee there being an exhibition on the day you are walking of course, but if you notice that one is being held, I think you will be impressed by the visual impact and diversity of local talent. When you leave the library, turn left and follow the pavement, so that the precinct and Long Eaton Green are to your right, then just continue with the shops and offices on your left to the canal bridge.

If you are staying on the towpath, then a summer afternoon will enable you to see the red admiral and peacock butterflies swarming around the buddleia thickets, thriving alongside the wall on your right. Continue then along the towpath, retracing your steps to Sandiacre and the Bridge Street car park.

Radcliffe on Soar Power Station

The immensity of the cooling towers is best appreciated when the motorist or coach passenger leaves the M1 motorway by the 'Nottingham South' exit and takes the Clifton road which also connects the motorway with Wilford and the centre of Nottingham.

The Radcliffe on Soar power station was commissioned during the second half of 1987. The site covers some 384 acres with the lower building screened in places by stands of closely planted pine trees. The total cost of construction was in the region of £8.5 million and the power station recognised as among the largest and most effective throughout the country.

Twenty thousand tons of coal are burnt every twenty hours and the Babcock and Wilcox boilers produce an astounding two tons of steam per second, the total output of which supplies energy for the four 500 MW turbine generators.

The end product, electricity, is then fed into the Trent Valley's super grid at a rating of around 400,000 volts.

Long Eaton

Situated between the River Trent and the M1 motorway, Long Eaton was originally a Welsh settlement until 603 when the Danes gained control and remained until 874.

When the Domesday Book was being compiled, the Anglo Saxons called the settlement Aitone which meant 'town beside the water'.

The Parish Church of St Lawrence may have been rebuilt on or around a chapel or Saxon place of worship, but the Norman influence has remained. The chancel boasts a fourteenth century window and the south doorway is fitted with three types of moulding, beat lead, circular chain and double billet.

On the west side of the town a public school, Trent College, surrounded by forty acres of gardens and playing fields, has for long been predominant in the training of engineering skills and chemical tuition with its physical and biological laboratories well to the fore.

The town has both an open air and enclosed swimming pool at the Grange Park and West Park respectively. There is also a stadium where greyhound and stock car racing has attracted thousands of enthusiasts throughout the best part of this century.

Football, cricket, bowls, hockey and tennis are also played at West Park (137 acres) and Sawley Park (8 acres).

Long Eaton Mills

These tenement mills can best be appreciated by standing on the towpath of the Erewash Canal or the Derby Road bridge which spans the waterway. The four storey buildings at the beginning of this century employed half the working force of this industrial town.

Designed with the intention of providing rented space for several separate firms, the buildings attracted many businessmen, some with minimum capital, but signing agreements which ensured that they shared the cost of power, electricity and business rates etc.

The mills are typical of those built for the lace industry and have been designed with many cast iron windows to provide adequate lighting for the employees and also turreted, brick staircases which provided the maximum floor space required to cope with the hustle, bustle and general productive activities that took place either side of the long machines.

The building beside the canal as one approaches the Derby Road bridge is called collectively Bridge Mills and was completed in 1902. On the other side of the bridge is a derelict coal wharf and the West End Mill (1882) and Whiteleys Mill (1883 respectively).

To view them from street level you need to take the steps immediately left when you pass beneath the bridge, cross the bridge and turn first left into Leopold Street. Halfway down on the right is Stanhope Mills, a single storey building with extensions added since it was completed in 1907. Farther along on the right are the bulkily impressive Harrington Mills (1885). The first turn on the right will take you along Stanhope Street with the Engineering Works on your left (1886) and Stanhope Mill to your right. At the end of Stanhope Street turn right and walk back to the canal bridge.

Further down the canal towpath and on your left as you are approaching the lock-gate stands an electricity generating station (1903) and the solid walled Alexandra Mills (1905).

Just past the lock are the Edward Mills (1909 and Victoria Mill (1906).

Across the canal is the green-space, West Park, where local folk stroll or exercise their dogs and a small fair or 'Wakes' is held in midsummer.

The Erewash Canal

The waterway extends for twelve miles therefore the towpath walker should be thinking in terms of checking the bus timetables for Long Eaton or Langley Mill, its termination points or travelling with friends and using two cars; one to be parked at one destination, the second at the other and walking to the car parked farthest from their starting point.

It is an interesting and variable walk, providing one can accept the small industrial estate depots fringing the towpath around Ilkeston, as readily as one can savour the evening sunlight enhancing the meadows and reedy backwaters around Stanton Gate.

For a brief history of the canal we need the date 1777 when an Act of Parliament was passed allowing for the construction of the waterway and recognition of its purpose for transporting coal from the nearby collieries to the River Trent.

The consignments of fuel not ordered by Nottingham's coal merchants were transported to Leicestershire and Northamptonshire when the canal was completed in 1779.

In the nineteen twenties the canal became derelict and sycamore, willow, alder, reed and sedge colonised the wharves and barge turning points. A few years ago when I walked the towpath from Langley Mill two rotted barges were discernible in shape but covered by reeds and yellow flowering iris.

In 1983/84 the Erewash Borough Council included the canal into its environmental scheme which also involved sanctioning the designation of three conservation areas within walking distance of Sandiacre. Thus the towpath was resurfaced, trees and shrubs planted along the bank and seats were provided at interesting and appropriate sites.

The canal today is well used by leisure craft and narrow boat enthusiasts and few are the summer evenings when one fails to see narrow boats passing through the road bridge lock at Gallows Inn, Ilkeston, where in the pub itself is a corner with paintings of narrowboats and local canal scenes tastefully displayed around the walls.

13. Around Attenborough

The Route: Nature Reserve Car Park – The Strand – Banks of the Trent – Attenborough Church

Start: Nature Reserve Car Park

How to Get There

By Car: From Nottingham or Derby along the A453. Situated between Long Eaton and Beeston. Signposted 'Nature Reserve'.

Duration: 2 – 2.5 hours

Distance: 3.5 – 4 miles

Maps: Land Ranger 129 – 1:50 000 or Nottingham (South West) Pathfinder 1:25 000

The Walk

Leave the car park by the entrance through which you have just driven with the church on your left, cricket ground to your right. And both intersected by an interesting backwater. When you reach the road turn right but do keep an eye on the incoming traffic.

Walk up The Strand. Some lovely cottages on the left there. Go through the tubular gate at the far end and proceed along the lane between the hawthorns, willows and alders with the leased gravel extraction lakes of the Attenborough Nature Reserve either side.

A quiet walk will reveal some interesting bird sightings, particularly to the right, in and around the thickets fringing the elongated stream or backwater.

When you reach the pylon bridge, pause to take in the scene across the water and the hilly fields beyond. The aquatic area to your left is known as The Works Pond where some of the gravel extraction barges are

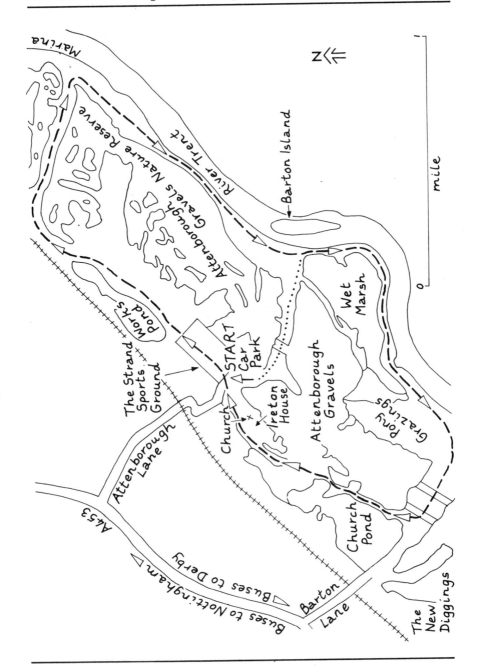

moored and proceed from.

Walk then along the sand track through the willow woods where, if you are out alone in the early morning, you may glimpse a fox hunting for bird fledglings or small mammals. Blackthorn thickets fringe the track as you are nearing the railway alongside which you should continue to where another track leads down from the railway crossing. Turn right again sharing this track with the strollers heading towards the River Trent. Between the thickets of hawthorn, alder and willow you will glimpse coots, tufted duck and mute swans, the latter perhaps feeding on the aquatic weed with necks submerged.

Where the lane converges with the rough ground and the riverside path, turn right again but pause to take in the flotilla of cruisers and long boats moored between here and Beeston Weir. Another interesting route ahead with a choice of yachts, cruisers, Canada geese and a rich variety of waterfowl.

In midsummer, do not regard every darting and swooping bird as a swallow or sand martin, because these sandy banks are nesting sites well favoured by kingfishers which nest in the small holes that are easy to define. One year eleven pairs of kingfisher nested between Beeston Weir and Barton Island. I mention this as an indication of just how popular these sand banks are.

Where the path and river bend you may gain some good sightings of cormorants, Canada geese and the mute swans, a few non breeding birds of which flock here to moult each summer. Eventually you'll meet with a path leading off between the gravel pits to your right. If you wish you can take this path back to the car park. But ahead is an interesting route and about another hours steady walking.

To your left now is Barton Island with a chalet or two and Sea Scouts' premises intact. To your right a backwater locally known as The Wet Marsh which, in my opinion, has been too well cleared of its aquatic cover and vegetation and should have been left alone. However a pair of mute swans breed there alongside great crested grebe and a variety of visiting gulls and terns. Those upright posts and the remains out by the far hedge are also used as perches by kingfishers, particularly during the summer months.

When the gravel extraction operations were first underway some forty or fifty years ago, the remains of a Roman encampment was discovered below the gravel layers of what is now The Wet Marsh.

When you reach the next path leading off from the right, take it noticing an arm of the Erewash meandering over to the left and try to envisage the dairy farm that was operational here until the nineteen sixties.

I recall some thirty years ago opening a gate and wending between the red hides of herded Shorthorn cows grouped in the yard for milking. Today only a scant few traces of the farm can be denoted. The gravel extraction water to your left carries a collective name 'The New Diggings'.. Eventually they will probably extend to the edge of Long Eaton.

Continue along the track, but before reaching the second pylon bridge, turn right using the spire of Attenborough village church as your guide for it should be rising above the trees before you. Still the aquatic scene either side, birds, insects, and water vegetation, but where this track ends you will find yourself on the gravel drive and by the livestock enclosure of the privately owned Ireton House.

In the stableyard enclosure are usually guinea fowl, peacocks, rabbits etc. The old house on your right there has a history dating back before the time of Oliver Cromwell and I have devoted a few paragraphs relating to its most colourful occupant in the following section.

Beyond the entrance gate is a turn, but for the bus, walk straight ahead over the railway crossing then turn left for the main road. To reach the car park you need to walk the tight bend by-passing Attenborough Church, which you may find worth an exploration. The pine trees here are the regular roosts of a pair of tawny owls that can sometimes be heard fluting in the early winter's dusk. Turn right again, keeping an eye out for cars coming around the tight bend. The Church and Standard Field, about which I have included a note in the next section, should be on your right. At the gateway on your right you need to turn onto the waterside footway, for you will no doubt have already recognized the car park, with the strollers, anglers and people feeding the waterfowl.

A Brief History of Attenborough

Situated between Beeston and Long Eaton the village of Attenborough carries documented evidence of a small monastery existence.

The church has retained a medieval door and 12th century tombstone which has been hung in the porch. The house by the church is associated with the visits of Oliver Cromwell who stayed at the invitation of Colonel Ireton, fighter for 'the cause', and eventually to become Cromwell's son-in-law. The field at the back of the church is called Standard Field and where, local historians insist, Colonel Ireton raised his standard during the Civil War.

The christening records of Oliver Cromwell's grand- daughter are displayed inside the church and in the churchyard is a communal grave where about 50 casualties of the Chilwell Ordnance Depot explosion were buried. The explosion occurred in 1918.

The present Parish Clerk is a lady and local historian whose ancestors have maintained that same position for more than 300 years.

The cricket and football ground alongside The Strand were bought collectively and Attenborough also hosts a tennis and bowls club, while primary, secondary and preparatory schools serve the educational purposes of the children in this adaptive community.

An Apparition on Standard Field

Over the years young equestrians saddling or feeding their ponies grazing Standard Field claim to have seen a 'cavalier type' figure walking the gentle slope. Those types of people who tend to keep an open mind have explored the possibility of this 'figure' being the apparition of Colonel Ireton, although he was of course a Roundhead, hence my usage of the term 'cavalier type'.

Then, from a young man cycling along the A453 at around five thirty on a summer morning, I was given an account of him freewheeling around the bend near the Chilwell Ordnance Depot when he saw a man "who looked as if he had been to a fancy dress party, standing on the pavement before taking a stride or two towards Attenborough village,

Attenborough in February

causing my informant to swerve swiftly aside. As he did so, the cyclist looked over his shoulder and shouted to the man, telling him to take more care when he was crossing the road.

The cyclist continued: "As he walked across the road looking neither left nor right, I noticed that the man was tall, bearded and had a cloak draped over his shoulders, wide trousers and was wearing high boots." Here it is worth noting that Ireton House and Standard Field are pretty well in direct line with the spot at which this near collision between the cyclist and the distinguished apparition took place.

Henry Ireton

Born at Ireton House in 1611 Henry Ireton was a staunch Parliamentarian who, after attending a defence committee formation held in Nottingham in 1642, joined the Parliamentarian army and became one of its most senior officers.

A distinctive and formidable adversary on the battlefield at Edgehill, he was wounded in the face and thigh at the battle of Naseby, but eluded his captors and appeared with full colours at the siege of Bristol in 1645. The following year he married Bridget, the daughter of Oliver Cromwell. Known as a man who kept his thoughts to himself, he lost no time in being appointed as one the judges, when Charles I was arrested, and placed his name and seal upon the death warrant.

In later years he joined Cromwell's campaigns in Ireland and died there 'of swamp fever' in 1651. His body was taken to Westminster Abbey but, with the Restoration in 1660, it was exhumed along with that of Cromwell and publicly displayed until sunset on the Tyburn Gallows.

The heads of both Henry Ireton and Cromwell were then severed and displayed on spiked railings outside Westminster Hall, while their bodies were reburied beneath the gallows.

The Robin Hood Way

This long distance recreational footpath was the brain-child of Christopher Thompson, whose enthusiasm in getting the project underway admirably persuaded members of the Nottingham Wayfarers Rambling Club to plan and map out the route in commemoration of the Club's Golden Jubilee year in 1982.

This resulted in a footpath extending for some eighty-eight miles from Nottingham Castle into the heart of the Robin Hood country.

An informative book 'The Robin Hood Way' can be obtained at tourist information centres and leading bookshops in Nottingham, Mansfield and Derby. Fully illustrated and with route maps, it covers one hundred circular walks. So if you are resident hereabouts or a rambling enthusiast staying over for a few days, do read a copy. It is my guarantee that you will not be disappointed.

14. Exploring
Colwick Country Park

The Route: Towards Colwick Sluices – West Lake – Original Hall Lake – Colwick Hall

Start: Car Park by the Rangers' Portacabin

How to Get There

By Car: From Derby to Nottingham along A52. But at the roundabout linking the A612, follow around onto the B686. Colwick is eventually to the right and is well-signposted.

By Bus: Service No.20 from Victoria Centre, Nottingham. Check the times. Alight at 'The Starting Gate' and cross the road to the pub side, noting the signposts.

Distance: 2.5 – 3 miles

Duration: 2 hours at a leisurely pace

Maps: None needed really, as just waterside paths to follow. But Pathfinder SK62/72 1:25 000 are appropriate.

Added Note: In uncertain weather carry waterproofs as there is little shelter until you are two-thirds of the way around.

This is a circular walk around the lakes and marina banks of a tract of land which was once part of the Colwick Hall estate which, since the last war, was extensively worked for gravel extraction before being purchased by the Nottinghamshire County Council and developed into a country park.

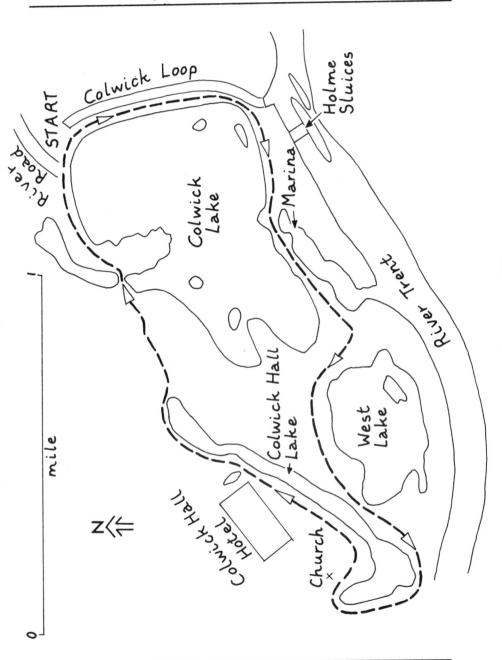

The Walk

Leaving the car park you can take whichever direction you wish, but the route described here is that most often used by myself and friends.

From the car park turn with the Rangers cabin to your left and proceed around the lakeside with Holme Sluices prominent beyond the river bank.

The Canada geese and feral grey lags breed on the islands and a pair of mute swans nest annually on the small willow island, while displaying and chasing the flock of non breeding swans from their territory.

Eventually to the left you will pass the backwater of the River Trent which is now used as a marina. If you have a camera it is worth pausing to line the moored craft in your view-finder, because scenes such as this make an interesting photographic study.

Where the main lake ends bear right so that the West Lake is to your left. Just cross the grass rounding the lake and keeping it to your left. Most local bird enthusiasts know this to be a good water for attracting 'saw-billed' duck species such as the merganser and gooseander during the autumn and winter months.

Where the West Lake rounds completely, continue across the grass and on reaching the riverside path swing right with the river to your left.

Common terns and a variety of gulls can sometimes be seen over the river, while to your right is a long tract of woodland that has seen better days in that it has been taken over largely by fast regenerating sycamore.

In the long hollow is the original Colwick Hall lake and its island at this near end. Continue round with an arm of this water to your right and keep bearing right so that you cross the arm, then turn through the gate near the church. This is a quiet sylvan corner.

The lake is now to your right and you take the path between the trees. So for the bird enthusiast there is a variety of woodland and waterbirds to be seen. Besides woodpeckers, treecreeper and nuthatch, there are usually a few water rails thrusting among the runnels, reeds and sedges; particularly in the winter months.

Eventually to the left you will see the walls of the Colwick Hall Hotel which was formerly Colwick Hall with an interesting history and the inevitable 'White Lady' apparition. Its basic history I have relayed in the attached paragraphs.

Where the woodland walk ends continue through the gate and across the grass with the water to your right, taking in the relaxed atmosphere until you reach the car park.

The Musters of Colwick

Colwick Hall was originally the home of the Byron family who eventually sold the ornate country house to one Sir James Stonehouse Bart. Its next owner was Sir John Musters, son of a wealthy London grocer. This branch of the Musters family was granted arms in 1680 by Sir William Dugdale, Garter, King of Arms, though whether he instantly connected Sir John to the Musters (already well established in Nottinghamshire) is difficult to discover.

Sir John Musters eventually acquired Tower Place in Middlesex where he died in 1689, although he was buried at Colwick where his monument in the church stated that, according to a certain Mr Camden, he was descended from the de Monasteriis (Musters) of Yorkshire.

Sir John's eldest son, also named John, married Millicent Mundy, so that surname was entered in the family records. We find that this John's grandson, Mundy Musters, was a very generous man who, during the Christmas of 1762, provided his tenants with two quarts of ale, a stone of beef, four bushels of wheat and as much fuel as they required. On New Years Day 1763 each tenant was given half a guinea.

Mundy's son, another John, had Colwick Hall refurbished and rebuilt in 1776. His wife Sophia, the daughter of a chamber maid, painted the east window of Colwick Church. Sophia was regarded as a 'young woman of considerable beauty' which is obviously why she became a lady in preference to a chamber maid.

This couple had a son also named John, who in 1806 changed his surname to Chaworth by Royal licence, but had reverted to Musters again by 1823.

John married Mary Ann Chaworth who, history records, did not find herself enjoying the relationship and suffered a nervous breakdown, which was not improved by the presence of a rioting and looting mob who on 10 October 1831 ransacked Colwick Hall. Understandably terrified Mary fled from the house and hid in a nearby shrubbery, despite the pouring rain which was thought to have been the cause of her feverish condition and untimely death.

Two other locations, Wiverton Hall and Annesley feature from hereon within the family history, with Colwick Hall being sold in 1896, eventually to be purchased by the Nottingham Corporation who designated its surrounding acres as 'public pleasure grounds', although they bore little resemblance to the recently established water park around which you have just rambled.

The Trent Valley Way

This is a walking route of some eighty-four miles extending from Attenborough and Thrumpton, dependent on which side of the river you intend to begin – to West Stockwith where the Chesterfield Canal meets the tidal section of the Trent on the far north eastern side of the county. Established in 1989 to commemorate the centenary of the Nottinghamshire County Council 'The Way' becomes one route at Clifton Bridge and passes through Trent Bridge, Holme Pierrepoint, Gunthorpe, Newark, North Leverton and Gringley on the Hill, where glimpses of the River Idle and a stroll along the towpath of the Chesterfield Canal will serve to further enhance a day's exploration of that area.

If you choose to explore the Trent Valley Way in sections and travelling by car, do call at the North Leverton Windmill which is a four-sail tower mill built between 1813 and 1818. Splendidly conserved and open to visitors every day but Tuesdays from two until five p.m.

The mill is still used for grinding purposes by local farmers and smallholders.

Guide books and leaflets on the Trent Valley Way are available from local bookshops and libraries.

15. Around Holme Pierrepont

The Route: Adbolton Lane or Country Park car park – National Rowing Course – Finger Ponds – River Trent footpath – Holme Road – Grantham Canal – Adbolton Lane

Start: Either the No.85 Bus Terminus Adbolton Lane or the Country Park car park.

How to Get There

By Car: From Derby along the A52 (A6011). Turning first left after bridge crossing the canal at Gamston. This could be included with the Bassingfield Walk.

By Bus: No.85 from Nottingham Market Square. Board at the opposite end to the Council House. Frequent service even on Sundays when in the summer, passengers can alight at the Country Park. To check the times; Tel: Nottingham 503665

Distance: 5 miles approx.

Duration: 3.5 – 4.5 hours

Maps: Nottingham SK63/73; 1:25 000 or Pathfinder 834.

Note: If conditions are doubtful, carry waterproofs for there is very little shelter.

The Walk

If you start from the Adbolton Lane bus terminus, you need only walk ahead with the hedge on the left and continue left at the junction with the Skylarks Home for the Disabled again on your left and the Green Acres Mobile Home site a field or so away to the right. Nor need you be facing oncoming traffic all the way, for where the trees fringe the road the path swings slightly left and diverts through a pleasant few hundred yards of thicket and ground layer shrubs before it rejoins the road.

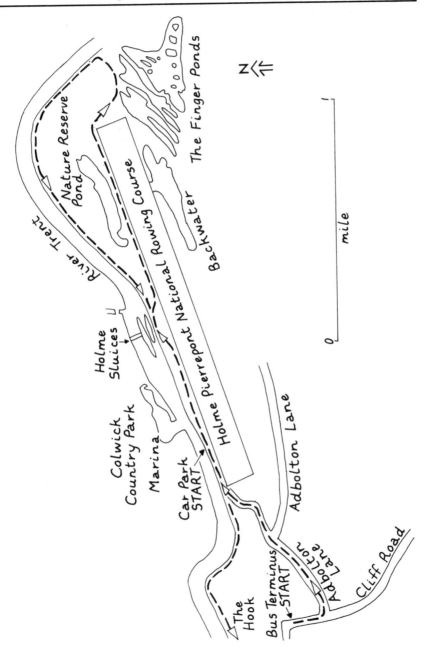

Where the road forks take the slip road on your left and within another hundred or so yards you will be entering the gateway of the National Watersports Centre and Country Park. Keep the National Rowing Course to your right and walk its length. Surrounding this well televised stretch of water is 270 acres of angling lagoons and picnic areas, while alongside you a power boat racing event or international regatta could be taking place.

Gulls, herons, Canada geese and mute swans you may see flying from one feeding ground to another. When you notice a pool over on your left, then divert along its bank until you reach the rapids of the slalom course where, if you are lucky a team of kayaks maybe competing, in yet another colourful event.

The slalom course for rafting and canoeing was created at a natural fault in the ground levels. One enthusiast claims there is a difference of about one hundred feet in contour depths. Thus by opening a sluice at the highest point the canoe rapids are achieved and the water cascades back into the river.

As you walk the hillocks or grass banks still keep the rowing course to your right remembering that to be walking on grass is to be walking on a cushioning form of electricity, which the environmentalists insist is relaxing for the mind.

When you reach the end of the rowing course swing right and after its span, follow one of the several paths through the hawthorn and elder thickets to have a look at the gravel extraction area, known locally as The Finger Ponds.

The anglers know this to be a good pike water! The bird watchers also know it as an excellent place for seeing waders, waterfowl and small birds of the thicket. But there is also scope for the photographer, especially as the spire of the Holme Pierrepont church makes an interesting study beyond the channels and islands.

Holme Pierrepont Hall can also be glimpsed among the trees. A privately owned Tudor manor house with a ghost that occasionally slams doors, the building houses several fine art and furniture collections.

April daybreak: the Finger Ponds, Holme Pierrepont

This is the farthest point of the walk so bear left now through the scrublands to the bank of the River Trent, then turn with the river on your right and follow the path for about a mile towards Nottingham.

Just by the lock house are the Holme Sluices and behind them the Colwick Country Park; it would make sense to have a bridge across the river spanning these two areas, but despite recent negotiations the relative authorities have failed in sanctioning this worthwhile amenity. A few hundred yards beyond the Sailing Club on your left is a pond known as The Old Trent Pool. Probably this was a minute section of the original river bed.

The Hook is the acreage of grass to your left, so called because it meanders with the course of the river. If you look across the grass and see a gap or gate in its bordering hedgerow, then cross to this and into Holme Road where you should cross and continue down the left-hand pavement to its junction with Trent Boulevard.

Cross with care and follow the pavement corner round to the left.

You should now be on Radcliffe Road. As a pointer check that you have a shrubbery on your left and pelican crossing to the right. But do not cross. Continue by the shrubbery and hawthorn hedge until you reach the hand gate that takes you onto the towpath of the Grantham Canal.

Being unnavigable, this stretch of water provides habitat for moorhens, coot, mallard and a resident pair of mute swans. In the autumn the occasional kingfisher pays a visit despite the proximity of the suburban scene.

At the next gate turn left along by the fence over the road to the next gate, where another short canal walk awaits. At yet another gate, by the telephone kiosk, turn with the kiosk on your right and walk down the snicket to Rutland Road which you need to cross then go along one of the roads opposite. Turn right onto Trent Boulevard and follow this into Adbolton Lane, which will take you back to the bus terminus or the National Water Sports Centre where your car is parked.

16. Around Bassingfield:
The Wildlife Enthusiast's Walk

The Route: Bassingfield Lane and Bassingfield – Cotgrave Place – Grantham Canal

Start: Bassingfield Lane (off the Gamston Lings Bar Road

How to Get There

By Car: Follow the A52 (A6011) from Derby and through Nottingham to West Bridgford, then turn right at the Gamston-Lings Bar roundabout, first left, then left again into Bassingfield Lane.

By Bus: From Nottingham Broadmarsh Nos.22 – 22B – OR23. Check the times and ask for the Lings Bar Layby. On alighting, walk up the narrow cutting to your starting point.

Distance: 2.5-3 miles

Duration: 2.5 hours, but longer if watching wildlife behaviour etc.

Maps: O/S Pathfinder 1:25 000 Sheet 63/73

Additions: Binoculars, camera and wildlife recognition book for wild flowers, butterflies etc.

The Walk

Your starting point, Bassingfield Lane is the territory of a dog fox. One of his vixens is usually 'earthed' in the long bank between the Lings Bar

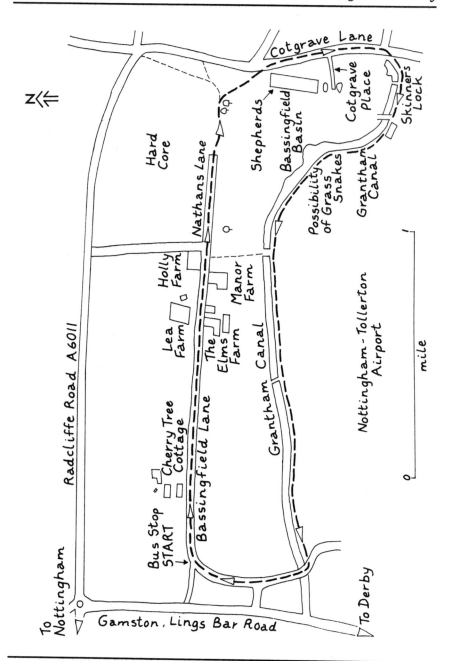

road and the lane. A friend out at six one May morning saw this fox crossing with a partridge clamped tightly between his jaws and, if you are walking quietly around this time of year, you may be similarly rewarded.

You need to be facing oncoming traffic, so walk on the right-hand side by the holding and cottages. Rooks feed across these fields, particularly on winter afternoons. Black headed and common gulls occasionally join them.

If you are carrying binoculars, then scan the rough pasture for in mid-winter you may see flocks of redwings and fieldfare; in the summer a few lapwing or partridge, linnets, yellow hammers, chaffinches. Scatterings of reed buntings and blue, great and long tailed titmice will be glimpsed feeding throughout the hedgerows or perched along the telegraph wires.

Kestrel and sparrowhawk will in all probability be quartering the fields and hedgerows. Or you may see one or other of these predators perched along the wires overlooking a dung heap or discarded pile of hay and straw waiting for small rodents and birds to appear.

The farms, The Elms, Lea, Holly and Manor are close together and on the right at the time of writing is a deserted farm – but a fine example of barns, stockyards and stables that for the standing by the entrance make an interesting study. Swifts and swallows nest in these old buildings and house martins beneath the eaves. Notice the splendid trees hereabouts and the vines covering the cottage walls.

The cart track off to your right leads you over the farmer's bridge to the towpath of the Grantham Canal. But you will be returning that way so for this walk keep on by the cottages.

At the T-junction progress directly along Nathans Lane with the Lombardy poplars either side. The lane becomes a bridleway which crosses on arable field to the horse paddocks with yourself stopping perhaps to admire the animals, but resisting the temptation to feed them.

Eventually the paddock on the left gives way to the refuse tip where much hardcore is piled. I mention this to illustrate the point of how quickly a land tract can be changed.

Twenty or so years ago there was a gravel extraction lake visited regularly by golden eye pochard and tufted duck and I once watched a pair of mute swans fiercely chasing off a group of younger swans here. Eventually the path divides alongside the old oak tree and mature ash in the hedgerow to your right. A corner section of the hedge has been removed, but there is a redundant stile alongside the oak.

If the weather is damp or wet, then continue to the next gate leading onto the 'B' road and turn right to follow the hedge along. In comfortable conditions, however, take the path across the centre of the field which, I think you will agree, is well defined, whether there are crops or stubble. All credit then to the landowner! The birds most likely to be seen on these fields are snipe, lapwing, rook, jackdaw, partridge, pheasant and woodpigeon. Climb the double stile and be aware that the 'B' road is on the other side.

Turn right facing oncoming traffic, then walk the grass verge to the road junction. 'Chimes' of goldfinches may be feeding on the countless thistleheads in the uncultivated fields to your right.

At the sign 'Cotgrave 1.5', turn right noticing also the sign for 'Stragglethorpe' with the mileage blocked out and about which I have explained in the following notes.

Shepherds Restaurant I have also mentioned and as you are walking with this spacious hostelry on your right, I will recall my first visit on a winter night when the pub was about a quarter its present size and the landlady conversed with us, while she sat sewing at the bar. The fox mask on display then is at forehead height now and every conceivable nook and cranny or wall is crammed pleasantly with pictures, prints, horse harnesses, stuffed birds etc.

You need now to be walking the grass verge by the Cotgrave Place Golf and Country Club until you reach the ash trees and the canal. Cross the canal then turn right onto the towpath. This has been widened to allow vehicle access to Skinners Lock where the current resident, Mrs Bemrose, has lived for fifty-four years.

During the early part of the year, sheep and lamb rearing pens are a usual feature in the field to your left; in the hawthorn cutting pheasant

Winter at Skinner's Lock on the Grantham Canal

occasionally feed and such predators as the stoat, weasel and fox hunt for small mammals. On the far side of the next field notice the Dutch style open sided barn with its outbuildings and four or five shire horses, which make a welcome addition to the rural scene.

Mrs Bemrose and her husband were the third generation of canal workers to move into this lock-gate residence. The Skinners were the first occupants to be followed by the Waltons. The men were employed as lengthmen, trimming the hedgerows and inspecting the waterway for leaks. Each lengthman had a three-mile stretch of the canal to maintain.

There is a footbridge now over the canal at Skinners Lock, but Mrs Bemrose, still nimble in her eighties, prefers to use the plank bridge when she crosses the canal to collect kindle for the fire. The kindly lady has a fund of anecdotes concerning the waterway and its wildlife and is often seen to enthuse about the kingfisher or heron that settled before the cottage at first light, or the shire foal born a day or two previously. Notice the brook dividing the lockhouse garden.

Along the next long stretch of waterway you may see moorhen, coot, mallard and little grebe. Those five beeches on the opposite bank attract the occasional grey squirrel and here my friend Tony Stevenson watched one such mammal swimming the canal. This is also a good place to be looking for young tawny owls which perch in the tree branches and call to the parent birds, which from late May until the beginning of July will be coming in with food.

On frosted nights in the autumn and winter I have walked in the darkness here and stood listening to the owls fluting across the fields. A quiet walk along the long stretch may reward you with glimpses of a water vole, or a stoat or weasel, either hunting along the hedgerow or, less frequently, crossing the canal to hunt for voles or moorhen chicks.

When you come to the small lock-gate I should explain that the daffodils you might see flourishing in March and April are not 'wild daffodils', but were planted by an angler's wife to quietly commemorate the fact that her late husband loved this spot and spent a good deal of his time angling here. The wooded bend, known locally as 'the viaduct' may during the summer months provide you with the unusual sighting of a grass snake swimming below the canal surface and hunting for frogs or small fish.

Meanwhile you will undoubtedly glimpse or hear the summer visiting warblers, yellow hammers and corn buntings, while fluttering and displaying over the reeds or along the towpath could be several pairs of yellow wagtails.

Off to the right is a wide tract of arable land that reminds you of the Cambridgeshire Fens. Beyond it are the hangars of Tollerton Aerodrome, which, as well as an airport, is now a club for light aircraft enthusiasts, as those who walk this way on Sundays will have become well aware.

Notice the bunkers, still in tact across the fields. According to 'Mrs Bem' back there, this was once on active station during the war and once scheduled to become the East Midlands Airport.

The trees in the hedgerow here are oak and ash; the hedgerow thicket, hawthorn, blackthorn and elder. There are some delightful stands of reed, mace or sedge on the opposite side and just as you reach the

Tollerton Lane bridge, a grassy ledge provides anchorage for the resident pair of mute swans that nest there.

If you are a motorist then your car is hopefully just down the road from this bridge. But if you are a walker, who intends following the towpath to West Bridgford, then just continue, taking care when you have to cross the roads, particularly the fast Lings Bar Road linking Nottingham and Birmingham.

At West Bridgford, where the canal terminates, leave the path and walk down Radcliffe Road and over Trent Bridge, crossing to the Victoria Embankment side and catching any bus into the city.

Derby's walkers can alight at Broad Marsh and from there catch a bus home.

Notes on Bassingfield and Cotgrave Place

Now separated from its close neighbour Gamston by the fast Lings Bar road, Bassingfield was little more than a hamlet until after the Second World War.

Almost every able person worked at one of the four thriving farms which produced crops and dairy produce. In some parts of the hamlet only a wide field separated the winding lane from the Grantham Canal; colourful with its barge traffic and group of anglers. Fields of potatoes were picked by hand labour, the cows milked twice daily and ten or twelve acre fields ploughed by one man guiding a two horse team.

Nearby Cotgrave Place maintained sizeable pheasant coverts and like most estates throughout the county created artificial fox earths within the thickets to encourage vixens to breed litters, which in time provided sport for the local hunting fraternity.

The coverts of Cotgrave Place have for decades produced a strain of white pheasant, the last four individuals of which were believed to have been taken by poachers. Over of the last few years those who regularly walk the footpaths have witnessed the transformation of the Cotgrave Place estate from rich 'typically English' parkland into a 27 hole golf course, threaded throughout by a watercourse, but with the stands of oak and beech further highlighting the contours of the green, undulating landscape. The Golf and Country Club was officially opened on May 22 1991. The golf course is but the first phase of an interesting development which, when completed, will hopefully include an equestrian centre, jogging track, nature trail, bowling green and hotel. Just by the entrance to Cotgrave Place four cottages once lived in by the estate woodsmen and estate workers were converted into the popular Shepherds Restaurant with its extended car park and children's play area.

On winter nights, the sodium lighting literally highlights the splendour of the trees surrounding the car park. On one occasion, a tawny owl flew from the branches of a corner tree just as we were leaving the main entrance.

Around half past one on a winter morning a former landlady was completing a last chore before retiring when she found herself confronted by 'an old man with a grey beard'. As beards were traditionally worn by both the woodsman and gamekeeper, she probably saw the apparition of a man who had previously lived in one of the cottages on the site.

At the T-junction below Shepherds Restaurant is a road sign with an arm directing the traveller to Stragglethorpe; but with the number of miles intentionally rubbed out. This is obviously because the hamlet of Stragglethorpe is no longer in existence, for its few single lined cottages once stood where the spoil from Cotgrave Colliery is now heaped.

17. Around the Trent Hills

The Route: Old Mill Lane – Kneeton – Watsons Piece – East Bridgford

Start: Left hand side of the East Bridgford to Kneeton Road at the 'bridleway' sign

How to Get There

By Car: From Derby and Nottingham along the A52 turning left at Radcliffe on Trent onto the A46. East Bridgford is signposted.

By Bus: Service No.14: Monday-Saturday every hour from Nottingham Victoria. Sundays: every two hours. Destination: 'East Bridgford and Gunthorpe'.

Parking: Allowed in moderation on the wide grass verges by the Old Mill Lane to the walk. But the lane itself is not a public road, so parking is not permitted there.

Distance: 5.5 miles

Duration: 4.5 hours

Maps: 1:25 000 SK64 and SK74 1:50 000 Sheet 129

The Walk

The starting point for this walk is the Kneeton to East Bridgford road and you need to be thinking in terms of standing half way between the tower of the disused windmill and the last house in the East Bridgford parish. Your actual marker is the 'Bridleway' signpost and it is along this surfaced farm track you need to begin walking with the haw and blackthorn hedgerows either side.

On your right are the ruins of a six sailed windmill which was built in 1841 and survived as a working mill for sixty or seventy years. After falling derelict it was dismantled around 1938-39.

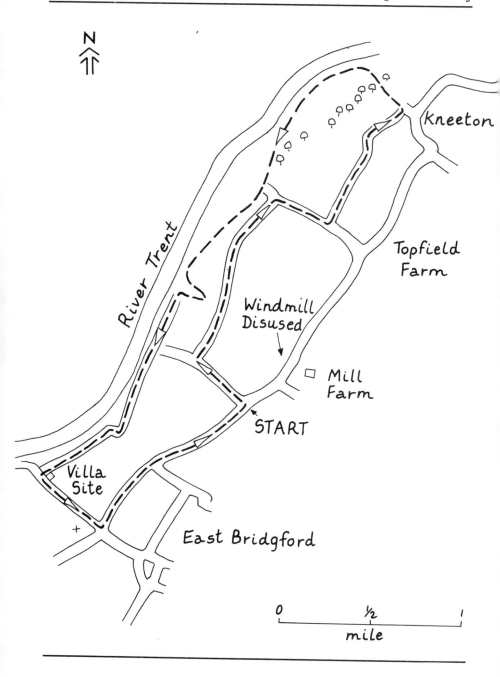

The track meets with Old Mill Lane and you need to take this, turning right and enjoying the greenery or the autumn colours dependent of course upon the season you've chosen for your walk. Enjoy too the views over the Dover Beck valley with Gonalston and Epperstone nestling low within the hills.

The member of the Ramblers Association who first introduced me to this walk relayed an account of this lane being used by shackled prisoners and mounted guards making their way across to Hoveringham Ferry. But where from there? Nottingham Prison? Eventually the lane narrows, but instead of continuing downhill, turn right at the waymarked stile set in a corner of the field. A steep hill beckons ahead with rabbits and pheasants feeding on the meadow grass and the hedge to your right. Notice the sizeable rabbit warren here and the various sizes of the rabbits as they move closer to the warren entrances. Several generations are usually evident here.

On reaching the stile at the top of the field, check that you are right by noting the metal field gate and head then along the farm track. There is a small open area, but you need to be looking at the next hedge and turning left with the hedge on your left. These fields are arable and therefore you should keep in single file. The village ahead is Kneeton.

Eventually you will meet with a low, trimmed hedge. Make your way around it and walk straight ahead. Walk for two hundred and fifty or three hundred yards then look for a gap in the hedge. Here the path continues to the opposite side of the hedge and leads to the corner of the field holding a metal farm gate. Having reached this, pass through the slip stile and turn down the narrow lane into Kneeton. On your left you will eventually see Church Farm with its tithe barn still intact. The little church nearby is St Helens.

On the church corner is a T-junction. Turn left but look over your right shoulder to the blacksmith's, a small and once-busy shop. Proceed down the hill using the ancient route to Hoveringham Ferry and looking at the somewhat eroded road surface with its stone and brick pavings purposely laid to provide a foothold for horses and wheelhold for the carts and dreys.

At the bottom of the lane is a wide field gate. Go through this, latching it with care, and follow the track down the middle of the field. To your left notice Toot Hill woods showing over the horizon.

The grassland here provides anchorage for many wild flower species and the elongated trough suggests a course of the River Trent. Probably some artefacts relating to Bronze or Iron Age Man are hidden beneath these grass and soil layers.

After by-passing the wind pump, you need to climb two stiles then, where the third meadow narrows between the river and the hill, use the old hawthorn tree as a guide marker and locate the stile in the thick hedgerow before you. Good place for seeing lapwing and snipe is this, especially if you are walking quietly in the early morning. After climbing the stile make slightly off to the right and follow the path around the bottom of the steep bank.

That land strip over to your right is Watsons Piece, frequented by foxes and woodland birds, including summer visiting warblers like the chiff chaff and blackcap. About 160 to 180 yards on from the stile continue up the steep bank and begin looking for the stile in the hedge to your left.

When you have climbed this stile, turn right and along the meadowside with the hedgerow on your right. In the field corner climb the three rail fence, turn left and climb the next fence. Then swing right with the hedge on your right and you are following the route alongside the River Trent.

Beyond the hill brow is a stile in the bottom corner of the field. Then go straight on noting the small birds, butterflies and varieties of daylight flying moth as you are approaching the wooded gulley. Take the steps now down the steep bank then up the opposite side. Fox and hare trails intersect the beds of stinging nettle and dogs mercury.

At the top of the gulley another stile awaits. Over you go into the corner of the field keeping the hedge to your right and beneath the electricity wires. Climb then the next stile, turn left along the bottom of the field, but ignore the farm gate. Just keep alongside the hedge with the river at your back. Another stile to be climbed and you are into an arable field.

Turn now towards the river then walk parallel to it while turning left along the hedge.

Go beyond the pylon and towards the copse and into it taking the path down the steep bank. Such places provide sanctuary for birds known to the watchers as "little brown jobs" – dunnocks, robins and wrens. But willow warblers will linger here and a bullfinch or two may occasionally be seen.

Follow the path left and downhill to the track in the gulley's base then climb the bankside track to the stile. Walk now with the hedge to your right and parallel with the river. Swing left around the next gulley, passing a footpath sign showing that you have a choice of three directions. But for this continue as before, hedge to your right and parallel to the river.

On your left is the Manor House and a stile opposite but with the fence removed when a disused wind pump was taken down six or seven years ago. Make use of the open access still keeping that hedge to your right. Go around the field corner to the next stile and over it towards the mobile home site. Time now to mention the viewpoints. The lock gate and weir are connected to the riverine village of Gunthorpe.

Over to your left is East Bridgford's Church of St Peter.

The next stile takes you onto the mobile home site, but there is a path through the centre. Follow the descending track to the edge of Trent Road which connects East Bridgford to Gunthorpe Bridge. On the site of the house, aptly called 'Moorings', stood a wharf with a ferry in operation until 1875 which is when the first bridge was constructed. The remains of this first bridge can be seen from the toll house on the far side of the river.

To have a look at the river you need to pass the seat then take the turn right. Notice the tree roots and an outcrop of gypsum here. To continue the walk, however, you return to the mobile home site, climb yet another stile and uphill along the signposted path on your left. Incidentally archaeologists have long recorded this as having been the site of a motte and bailey castle.

With the fence still on your left continue towards the tower of St Peter's Church. Away to your right on the hillside is East Bridgford Hall.

Yet another stile then along the path fenced on both sides to a lower stile. Continue then between the fences to the road on your left.

The path and road converge at the footpath signpost. Walk now towards East Bridgford where at the hilltop crossroads you turn left along Kneeton Road and the walk's end, or have a drink at 'The Reindeer' or 'The Royal Oak' which are to be found by taking the road ahead.

East Bridgford

The ridge-top village of East Bridgford also nurtures strong community spirit; with its current population of around two thousand, there is a primary school, medical centre, six shops, a post office and two pubs strung along the lanes and streets. Notice also the old farm buildings, barns and cottages still in good repair.

St Peter's church dates back some 1100 years and was ransacked by the Danes plotting the course of the River Trent. Once this band of looters had left, everyone in the settlement, in some way, helped in the rebuilding of the church to which the St Peter's Day celebrations are still bound. Originally the celebrations extended for a week of feasting and visiting the fair, but today the main theme revolves around a weekend at the end of June when families and friends reunite at the Saturday Horticultural Show. Youth organisations and The British Legion also hold displays then reassemble at St Peters for the services throughout Sunday. On the Monday cricket is played on the sports field.

The manoral family connection here was the Hackers who lived in the Old Manor House with various members supporting different sides during the Civil War. One staunch Parliamentarian, Francis Hacker, escorted Charles I to the scaffold, but after the Restoration was himself arrested and executed in 1660. The church incidentally displays a copy of the death warrant of Charles I.

A century later gypsum was being mined within the parish, a trade and industrial theme that existed until 1936.

Churchyard scene at East Bridgford

Gunthorpe

On this next walk you will catch several glimpses of Gunthorpe Weir and Lock halting and regulating the levels and flow of the River Trent which the Romans regarded as a 'Middle England Frontier'. Close by on the Fosse Way is the site of 'Margidunum' a Roman village station from which many mosaic tiles were taken and used as garden path and patio pavings after archaeologists declared them as of little monetary value when they completed their excavations twenty or so years ago.

The present Gunthorpe Bridge incidentally was opened in 1927 by the Prince of Wales who was a regular visitor to Nottinghamshire and the 'great' country houses in 'The Dukeries' twelve to fifteen miles to the north.

18. Around Ruddington and Plumtree

The Route: West Bridgford – Ruddington Village – Flawforth Lane – Plumtree Village

Start: Rushcliffe Leisure Centre, Boundary Rd

How to Get There

By Car: From Nottingham West Bridgford follow the A606 through West Bridgford, but looking for Boundary Road on your right

Parking: You are asked to use the 'Additional Parking' area at the Centre

By Bus: Check the Broad Marsh and Victoria Bus Station Hotline Nottingham 240000

Distance: 8 miles

Duration: 4 hours, if you are exploring the village

Maps: O.S. 1:50 000 sheet 129, or 1:25 000 sheet 53 & 63, or Pathfinder SK63/73

The Walk

Leaving the Leisure Centre entrance turn left and follow Boundary Road until you reach the junction where another left turn along 'Old Road' leads you past the Southern Cemetery and up to Wilford Hill.

Well documented by local naturalists are the beds of garlic mustard growing in the hedgerow and providing the necessary food source for the caterpillars of the orange tip butterfly which is the plant's best known host insect.

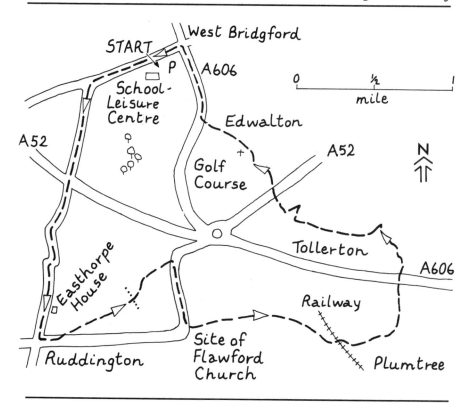

Notice too the beech trees as Old Road meets with the busy A52 dual carriageway at the bottom of the hill. You need to cross this fast road then go down the bank and through the hedge gap. Yes you are still on 'Old Road and heading around the side of Mickleborough Hill.

Near the hilltop is Hall Cottage and beyond it a turn half right and a descent along the bridleway. Where the way meets the road turn left, but ignore the sign to Ruddington Hall. What you need to be doing is swinging left onto the A60 Loughborough Road. You have half a mile or so of walking ahead, so I recommend you to take the pavement on the right as the opposite side narrows considerably. When you reach the traffic lights turn left into Flawforth Lane. That Regency style building to your left is Easthorpe House built early this century and now providing office accommodation for a private firm.

What you are looking for beside the hedgerow on your left is the signpost opposite the garden centre and the entrance to Silverdale Farm. Climb the stile, bear half right across the field and top the next stile. Keep in the same direction for four fields where, I should add, the occasional glimpse of a hovering barn owl enhances a walk in the late summer dusk.

In the last field you come to a row of willow trees and a ditchboard bridge which you need to cross. Turn left. Cross the next bridge and follow the hedge to the stream then turn right at the bridge. Notice the wooded hills screening the industrial sprawl of Nottingham to the north.

Cross the bridge and again follow the stream to your right to where it meets with a hedge gap. Go through this. Swing left and you will be back on Flawforth Lane. Follow the grass verge for six or seven hundred yards, until you reach the layby. Here the road swings sharply right. On the left is the site of Flawforth's former Church of St Peter, about which I have added a paragraph or so in the adjacent village notes.

Notice the bridleway just before you reach the layby. You should take this around two sides of the church and then swing left into the grassy track which continues through four fields. Eventually you will pass on the right a house. You need now the gate which leads out into a green lane which you should take until you reach the railway bridge. This was the Midlands Railway Company's important Nottingham to Melton Mowbray line opened in 1879. After its closure in 1968 it was, and still is, used for testing British Rail equipment. After the bridge you are looking for a right-hand bend and just beyond it a left turn. Check for the stile beside the gate on your right while keeping the hedgerow to your left.

After the next left-hand corner notice a stile in the field corner. After the stile swing slightly left and make for the end of the hedge metering from your left. Bear left now and follow the hedgerow along to Plumtree Main Road. Cross and walk left around the side of the house to the stile. After this there is another stile beside the ash tree. But do not climb it. Instead turn left and follow the hedge into the corner of the field.

The fence and ditchboard need to be crossed before you bear left across the field. Check that the footpath sign is awaiting you. You need to cross the Plumtree Bypass (A606) then continue slightly left across two fields, but using the corners and heading for the undergrowth to the left of those willows.

Climb the next stile then turn right alongside the stream. It is worth pausing to take in the tree species, for besides the willows, there are field maple, ash and beech. The hedge is blackthorn which burns white with blossom and later in the year Himalayan Balsam flowers along the bank.

A friend of long standing watches the rabbit colonies feeding in the dusk here, often until they are disturbed by a fox. And there is still a chance to see a barn owl hunting by daylight if it has a brood to feed.

Ignore the footpath over the brook, but look for the official footpath sign in the field corner ahead. Follow the hedgerow then to Tollerton Lane. Turn left here along the lane then turn right into Burnside Grove. At the roundabout turn right into Lothian Road then at its end left beside the playing field.

Fox cub about six weeks old; at this age, foxes still have blue eyes

At the end of the fence turn right beside the fields edge. Where the hedge swings to the right bear slightly left along the definable path to the footbridge beside the dogwood thicket and crab apple tree. Once over the footbridge follow the ditchside hedge, Continuing in the same direction over the field towards a lamp post. Close by is also a signpost.

Take care here for your route continues through the gateway and down the steps to the A52. Again I emphasize the fact that this is a fast and busy road, but after crossing, climb the embankment steps a few yards to your right.

Ahead is the Edwalton.Golf Course. Your route is beside the short hedgerow on the left and, where it swings left, cross to the second hedge on the left side of a green.

Here you need to turn right and proceed between the two plantations and the church spire ahead. You are looking now for the gateway to the right of this church which was founded by Robert Fitz-Randulph, Sheriff of Nottingham, Derby and Alfreton in the twelfth century. Some local historians believe that this was built as a penance to those involved in the murder of St Thomas a Becket.

Ruddington, Plumtree and Tollerton

The A60 and Kirk Lane lead into Ruddington village which is locally renowned for its pioneering work in the framework knitting industry. Several framework knitting workshops are still in tact and the Framework Knitting Museum on Chapel Street is worth a visit (Tel: Nottm. 846914). Another attraction is the Local History Society Museum based in St Peters Rooms, while it is worth pausing to look at some of the buildings in the village streets, for a few of these date from the 17th century.

Flawforth Church could have been built on the site of a Roman villa, for excavations once revealed sections of a mosaic floor. Alabaster statues have also been recovered and are now housed in the Nottingham Castle Museum. Smaller items are on display in Ruddington's Local History Museum.

A Saxon church was built on and around the base and at one time St Peters served the needs of the parishioners of five villages. It was however demolished during the 18th century.

The church in Plumtree village is St Marys. The doorway is of Norman design, but the greater parts of the building were added in the 13th and 14th centuries. Restorations occurred in 1873 when stones from the Medieval Trent Bridge were transported by sled and packhorse and used to strengthen the north aisle.

The Domesday Book records Tollerton as Troclaurstune. Tollerton Hall was originally Roclaveston Manor, this name being another variation of the name Tollerton. The Hall that we see today was built in the seventeenth century. Nearby St Peters church was believed to have been founded by the Normans, but around 1800 many sections were rebuilt using the Gothic style.

Twinkling-eyed local villagers are always keen to point out the squire's pew which was fitted with a marble fireplace!

19. Around Keyworth and Widmerpool

The Route: Keyworth Wolds – Widmerpool – Stonepits Plantation

Start: Centre of Keyworth Village

How to Get There

By Car: Derby to Nottingham picking up the A614 or A606 to Keyworth.

Parking: Off Bunny Lane in the village car park close to church and square.

By Bus: Number 14 or 54, but check Victoria and Broadmarsh bus stations or phone the Bus Hotline: Nottingham 824268

Distance: 5.5 miles approx.

Duration: 3 hours, but longer if exploring the villages.

Maps: Ordnance Survey 1:25,000 SK62 and 63 or 1:50,000 O/S Sheet SK129

The Walk

Leaving the centre of Keyworth village, head along Main Street by-passing the church of St Mary Magdalene, which in itself is well worth exploring.

You need to be going in the signposted directions of Wymeswold and Wysall until you reach the first right-hand bend, then continue down Lings Lane to a stile on your left and alongside the field gate. Having climbed this, swing diagonally right to go through the field gate.

Now bear left and climb another stile. Still continuing left, use the telegraph poles as your marker and go through the hedge gap to the left

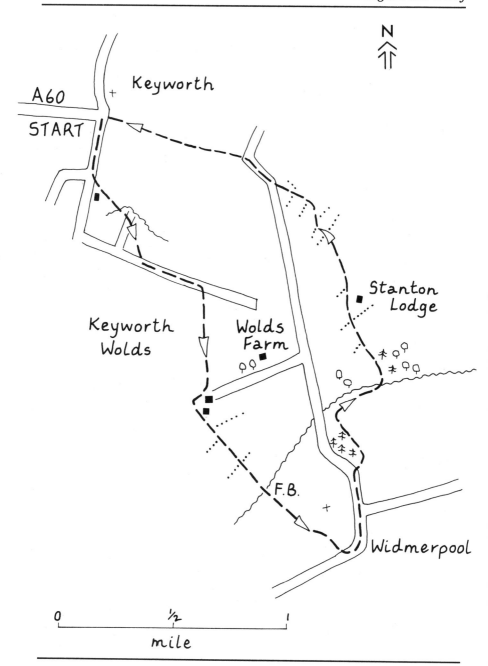

of them. Continue across the field to a stile and ditchboards on the far side. Cross these then bear sharp right into the right-hand corner of the field and out onto Wolds Lane, using one more stile and another set of ditchboards.

You will most likely flush hares and lapwings from these fields. 'Coveys' of common and red-legged partridge are also fairly widespread.

At Wolds Lane turn left, enjoying the landscape known as Keyworth Wolds which, before the Enclosures Act, was rough grazing land, uncultivated and in some parts heathland where warreners kept the rabbit populations in check.

On reaching the first stile to your right climb it and follow the field hedge on the left. Ahead is North Lodge Farm which should not go unnoticed because its owner has nurtured hedgerows, created a pond and planted such native tree species as the field maple, hazel (sadly depleted in Nottinghamshire), ash and oak.

Noting the two barns, follow the footpath signs around the nearest and alongside the second you will see the track and need then to turn left into the field.

Follow the hedgerow on your left until you arrive at the stile on the right of the metal field gate. Climb the stile and turn right. Walk across the field to the stile again to the right of two field gates. When you have climbed this, the hedge needs to be on your left and keep on, through a hedge gap and onto a field path.

Use now as a marker the tree ahead and bear to the left of it. On your right note the well managed Morris's Plantation which provides adequate habitat for small birds, pheasants, partridges and an occasional hare or fox. Notice too, the nearby stand of pines that occasionally attract goldcrests and greater spotted woodpecker. Now you are looking for the path which takes you around the right-hand side of the wood.

On your left you should arrive at a field gate and stile. But cross the track and turn right. Along here and a left turn will enable you to visit Widmerpool Church; its interesting features are included in the attached notes. Two really magnificent cedar trees have fallen in recent gales, but that church-surrounded-by-trees atmosphere is retained; or as long as future gales will allow.

Widmerpool church: centrepiece for a still-pleasant rural community

The track ahead takes you below the church but eventually you need to swing right to cross the Fairholme Brook. The fact that hawthorn, willow and black poplar branches overhang the water tells such wanderers as myself that this is a good place to be looking for a kingfisher, particularly during the autumn and winter months.

Beyond the brook you should continue through the hand gate onto Church lane, then turn right and follow the lane to the grass triangle. Bear left here. Then at the nexT-junction bear left again. Your route now is straight ahead, passing the Melton and Kinoulton Road and looking for the Widmerpool sign.

You now need the stile on your right. When you are over this, turn left and follow the hedge then at the corner turn right. The plantation (Stonepits) should be on your left.

At the corner turn left and cross the ditchboards. Then follow the field's edge beyond the end of the plantation to the end of the field beyond the pylon.

Turn right here with the Roehoe Brook to your left. Do not use the ditchboards leading into the wood. Instead walk over the next field using the pylon as your guide. A further 350 yards and you should come to a bridge crossing the brook, but go straight ahead, following the edge of the field. The wood should be to your right. Jays, all three species of woodpecker, nuthatch and tree creeper are the bird species you may glimpse here.

Do not hesitate at the sizeable hedge gap. Go through it and walk to the field corner then climb the bank.

Just before you reach the outbuildings of the nursing home, which was once Stanton Lodge, bear left to the stile. A right turn then brings you to the road. Turn left and at the road bend turn left again and through the hedge gap to your left. Bear slightly to your right and to the right of the telegraph wires.

The next section of the walk is best described as continuing across the paddocks and fields, noting the waymarked signs until you reach a small enclosure; sometimes called a corral. Go into this, then turn left and over the stile. The hedgerow should be on your left. Another stile awaits you, after which the hedgerow should be on your right.

The next stile takes you onto the grass verge. Climb it then turn right and walk along to Keyworth village and the beginning of your walk.

Widmerpool

Local historians regard Widmerpool as one of the oldest settlements in Nottinghamshire and have highlighted the possibility of its associations with the nearby Roman settlement *Vernemetum* (Willoughby) which was situated along the Fosse.

Widmerpool Hall, now used as offices by the Automobile Association

By the end of the twelfth century it was very much an estate village with the serfs working for the Lord of the Manor, one of whom was a John De Widmerpool noted for his Parliamentary attendances at York around 1333. There were also several disputes over land and boundaries which involved the Cromwells and Pierrepont families.

During the Civil War both Royalists and Parliamentarians passed through Widmerpool some to perish on the battlefield now known as Willoughby Fields. After one affray the original churchyard provided the burial spot for two of the soldiers who were laid to rest in an unmarked grave.

Widmerpool's strong social link with a Scots family, the Robertsons, became evident in the early 1800s and when this family acquired much land they lost no time in restoring the Elizabethan Manor house and church as well as rebuilding every cottage within the parish; a thought that comes to mind when today you locate The Old School House, the

Coach House and Gardener's Cottage. The oldest building, according to local records, is, however, Home Farm.

In 1836 the church spire was struck by lightning which smashed the windows and demolished the roof, but again the Robertsons were instrumental in the rebuilding of the church that we see today and which took about eight years to complete (1888-96).

By this time the Robertsons had changed their name to Robinson, but in what could by then have been accepted as their good family tradition, they had built Widmerpool Hall which also ensured that the estate village tradition was maintained at least until the nineteen fifties. When the estate was dissolved, the Hall, with its ornate furnishings, became the national training centre for the Automobile Association.

The Civil War Trail

Along with the several leaflets pressed into my hand when I entered the site of a colourful Muster, staged by members of the Sealed Knot Society to mark the 350th anniversary of the Siege of Newark, was one admirably researched and published by, I believe, the Newark Town Council with financial assistance provided by the Nottinghamshire County Council under their Tourism Initiative Scheme.

Planned as 'The Civil War Trail', this is a 'self-guided car and walking route', taking the interested local historian along the 23 miles from Nottingham to Newark and includes many quiet, but interesting villages. Each walk takes a minimum of around forty minutes to complete, and leaflets or further information can be obtained by contacting the Tourist Information Centres at:

16 Wheeler Gate, Nottingham, NG1 2NB; Tel (0602) 470661

or

Castlegate, Newark, Nottinghamshire NG24 1BG; Tel (0636) 78962

20. Around Hickling and Kinoulton

The Route: Hickling – Kinoulton Wolds and Gorse Vimy Ridge Farm – Grantham Canal

Start: Bridegate Lane, Hickling

How to Get There

By Car: A606 Nottingham to Melton Mowbray Road

Parking: Grass verge on Bridegate Lane – please do not block access to farm gates.

By Bus: Check at Broadmarsh Bus Station, Nottingham and note, in particular, the return times in the late afternoon or evening

Distance: 6 miles approximately

Duration: 2 – 3 hours

Maps: 1:25 000 O/S Sheets 62 and 63, 1:50 000 O/S Sheet 129, and also Pathfinder 1:25 000 sheets SK64/74

The Walk

Just west of Bridegate Lane is a signpost about 200 yards along the hedgeside and pointing South. Begin here by crossing the ditchboards and climbing the hedgerow stile, then working to the corner of the field.

The hedgerow needs to be on your left. Walk to the bottom of the field, climb the fence, turn half-right and notice ahead a gap in the hedge on the right. Make for this, cross the ditchboards and the stile, then make over to the far left-hand corner of this field.

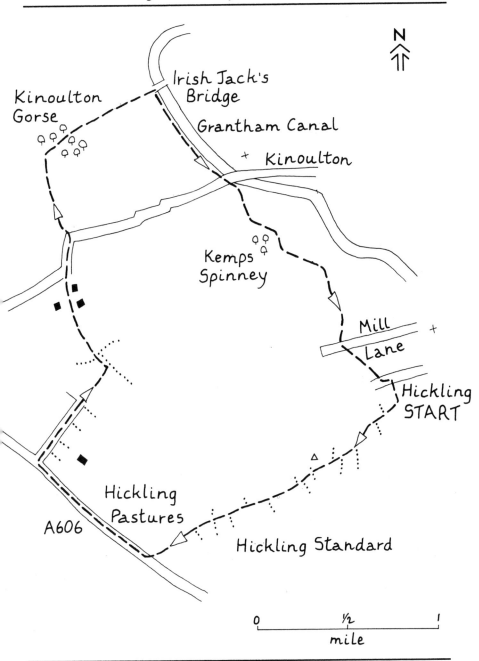

Kinoulton
Gorse

Irish Jack's
Bridge

Grantham Canal

Kinoulton

Kemps
Spinney

Mill
Lane

Hickling
START

Hickling
Pastures

A606

Hickling Standard

N

0   ½   1
mile

Next the long stile and across to the stile alongside the farm gate ahead. What you are looking for as you cross this field is a length of fence almost halfway from the top corner.

Use the stile over this fence then walk uphill to the far left-hand corner of the field. Having reached the hilltop look back and down onto Hickling village and the western edge of the Belvoir country. Over the fence then swing beside the hilltop hedge which you need on your left. This pastoral ridge is known as Hickling Standard and you are looking over Leicestershire and Nottinghamshire.

Beyond the next stile is an Ordnance Survey triangulation point, but in the field to your right. It informs you that you are 344 feet/105 metres above sea level. Onward and admiring perhaps the height and trunk width of those ash trees until you reach the field gate. Climb the stile alongside the gate and cross to the left-hand side of the next field, noticing the dead trees to your right where you might occasionally glimpse a tawny or little owl.

Another three fences are waiting ahead. Such walks as this I sometimes think should be called 'The Many Stiles Way'.

Eventually you can check your route for after topping the fourth stile there should be a pond. On again between the tall hedgerows across another stile and the ditchboards making for the far right hand corner of the field.

There is a double fence to your right. Climb this and turn left, up between the blackthorn thicket and to the corner of the field. Here you should meet with a signpost. Climb the stile and cross the ditchboards and you are on the grass verge of the Nottingham to Melton Mowbray (A606) road.

Turn right and walk in file for almost a mile. Face the oncoming traffic until after Bridegate Lane where the added luxury of a pavement awaits you. On the left-hand side of the road you will eventually see a wooden bus shelter and on the right a layby. Turn at the signpost just by this then use the ditchboards by this post and cross by the end of a sapling belt.

Ahead is a stile you need to climb and a hedgerow to your left. You will need to climb again, over the double fence distinguishable by the fact that its top rail was once a telegraph pole.

Through the field gate then and to the right of the water trough another pole topped fence beckoning. The path continues along the field edge and in front of Field Farm to the corner of the next field.

Turn left onto the bridleway and through the gate. You will have by now noticed that many of the fields hereabouts hold horses and ponies because this is hunting country; consequently stable yards and bridleways also prevail. This bridleway continues along the right-hand side of the field and through a gate where the hedgerow trails to the left.

Equestrian request. Although horses and ponies may come to the fence, please do not feed them

Use the hedgerow ahead which flanks the left-hand boundary of the next three fields to Lodge Farm. Stables again and the delightful aroma of fermenting manure. Then you are meeting with Kinoulton Lane and follow the grass verge along to the left. But although the lane turns right you are looking for the signpost to your left.

Go through the gateway and along the bridleway which continues between the hedgerow and a young plantation. Where the way swings to the left your route is to the right through the gate and between the hedgerows. Beyond the pylon is another gateway and the second plantation. Then a gate leading along the side of an arable field.

In the summer yellow hammers sing from the telegraph wires and corn buntings from the fence posts affixed into the hedge. Files of traffic over the fields to your left are using the Roman originated Fosse Way which connects the city of Bath to Lincoln.

At the end of the field another change of scene in that the track is bordered by hedgerows. Follow this to Kinoulton Gorse, probably a land tract once used for grazing the 'commoners' livestock, but having since regenerated to become mature woodland.

And again a now familiar pattern. Where the hedgerow to the left ends turn right through the gate and into the wood. Enjoy the glades, bluebells (in May) and bird song before you pause to take in the view of Borders Wood, the angular church marking the whereabouts of Owthorpe village, Colston Hall with its white frontage, the silo of Vimy Ridge Farm and in the distance Hickling church tower and splendid Belvoir Castle.

Continue then along the ditchside track taking in more of the Vale of Belvoir and as the bridleway nears Vimy Ridge Farm, the reedy bends of the Grantham Canal. The farm silo is made from concrete. Notice the weather vane and conical cap. A good place for roosting owls those outbuildings, particularly the occasional barn owl.

The route for the next few hundred yards is flanked by poplar trees. These were planted as a memorial to a landowner's son who, during the First World War, was killed at the battle for Vimy Ridge. Another version insists that one tree was planted for every officer killed in that battle – why not for every man?

The down-slope leads to Irish Jack Bridge which crosses the Grantham Canal. Irish Jack? He could have been the 'foreman navvy' in charge of the gang who constructed the bridge or a volatile bargee.

On the left is 'Devil's Elbow' a turning and bygone loading point for the bargees. House bricks, coal and flour were the main cargoes for this canal.

If you go down to the towpath and turn with Vimy Ridge Farm to your left, you will be off route, but the towpath is interesting for the field naturists' point of view. Between here and Owthorpe bridge the mute swan pair have occasionally to nest on the towpath because the dredgers have cleared all available nesting cover from their territory. I should add that the male or 'cob' of this pair, which have been nesting in the Trent Valley and adjacent areas since 1968, is exceptionally fierce and should not be closely approached if he's standing near the nest.

Your main route however is the towpath with Vimy Ridge Farm on your right. Coot pairs nest in the reeds, moorhen and little grebe are also attracted here and the mute swan pair are contrastingly placcid even with a brood of eight or nine cygnets in tow.

As you near Kinoulton village notice the aerial power lines with coloured spheres attached in a bid to prevent the swans and mallard from colliding with them. Concerned local villagers were the pioneers of this scheme.

For those who wish to walk it the canal towpath offers a pleasant route back to Hickling and glimpses of water voles or hovering kestrels from a towpath starred in places with early summer wildflower species.

But for the stile climbing enthusiast you need to cross the bridge bear to the right and cross to the right so that the canal is on your left. The signpost shows access through a stable yard and the paddock beyond. Do not be confused by the presence of gymkhana hurdles, but continue around the edge of this area then cross the field to its far right-hand corner.

At the wooden fence climb the stile and the same for the barbed wire fence. Then continue down the right-hand side of the next field, cross the footbridge to the gap in the hedge to your left. There is a stile you need to climb and ditchboards to be crossed.

Once across continue to the gate, then take the left corner of the next field. Beyond the next stile and the left-hand hedgerow alongside which you need to be walking is a barn close to Kemps Spinney.

Go to the corner of the field nearest the barn, then take a diagonal route across the next field to the greenway near the sad remnants of a hedgerow. Turn half right and cross the next field to the ditchboards which at the time of writing have the additional luxury of a handrail.

Cross the boards and the next small field making for the left side of the tall hedge. A stile fence next and you need to climb it then along the right-hand side of the field to another stile. Over this then and onto the farm track known as Mill Lane.

Cross the land and use the stile into the next field. The hedgerow should be on your left, but you are looking for the ditchboards about 18 or 20 yards from the far corner of this field, but still to your left. Cross the ditchboards and stile and in the next field make a half right turn and take a diagonal bearing to its opposite corner. There is a partially fenced pond and leaning willow tree here. Brace yourself for the gateway which is often muddy. Choose your place of purchase while remembering that the finest walker is the one who arrives back at the starting point with the least mud on his or her boots.

So here you are (hopefully) on Bridegate lane and perhaps wanting to see something of Hickling village and its basin before turning towards home. It should still be signposted but if not then Hickling is off to your left as you are standing with your back to the direction you have just walked.

Notes on Hickling and Kinoulton

The name Hickling derives from 'Echeling' by which this settlement was known to the Saxons.

St Lukes Church with its thirteenth century dome also safeguards the cover of a Saxon tomb, beautifully carved and estimated to be around

1000 years old. Into one of the interior church walls has been placed a 600 year old gravestone.

The best known part of Hickling to the 'outsider' is the basin where once bargees unloaded coal and their neighbours hauled agricultural products to the waterside for transportation and sale in the markets of Nottingham and Grantham. When it fell derelict, this section of the canal became an anglers' resort. In recent years, domestic ducks and geese have reared broods alongside coots, little grebe and the resident pair of mute swans, which annually hatch off a brood of eight or nine cygnets. The 'cob' or male of this pair incidentally was an immature bird in the early nineteen eighties when he was caught and leg ringed at Coventry in Warwickshire.

Kinoulton, which is a mile across the fields from the Fosse Way, probably originated from the settlement which was established around its twelfth century moated castle.

Some local historians insist that Archbishop Cranmer also lived in a palatial manor close by. The church that we see today is of late Georgian design, having been built around 1793. A plaque in the porch displays the fact that its benefactor and overseer was the Earl of Gainsborough. The former church, St Wilfrids, was abandoned during the eighteenth century, although its foundations and slate headstones can be seen for the removing (and replacing!) of a few divots of turf.

One story that has remained within this commuter belt village is that of the baker who made his ovens from the gravestones to the extent of his loaves being inscribed with the words 'In Loving Memory'.

At the eastern end of the village fronted by a small 'green' stands The Nevile Arms public house, a name commemorating the fact that the village was once part of the Gainsborough estate. The pub sign bears the coat of arms of both the Noel and Nevil families.

Explore the countryside with Sigma!

We have a wide selection of guides to individual towns, plus outdoor activities centred on walking and cycling in the great outdoors throughout England and Wales. This is a recent selection:

PEAK DISTRICT DIARY – Roger Redfern
An evocative book, celebrating the glorious countryside of the Peak District. The book is based on Roger's popular column in *The Guardian* newspaper and is profusely illustrated with stunning photographs. *£6.95*

I REMAIN, YOUR SON JACK – J. C. Morten (edited by Sheila Morten)
A collection of almost 200 letters, as featured on BBC TV, telling the moving story of a young soldier in the First World War. Profusely illustrated with contemporary photographs. *£8.95*

There are many books for outdoor people in our catalogue, including:

RAMBLES IN NORTH WALES
– Roger Redfern

HERITAGE WALKS IN THE PEAK DISTRICT
– Clive Price

EAST CHESHIRE WALKS
– Graham Beech

WEST CHESHIRE WALKS
– Jen Darling

WEST PENNINE WALKS
– Mike Cresswell

NEWARK AND SHERWOOD RAMBLES
– Malcolm McKenzie

RAMBLES AROUND NOTTINGHAM & DERBY
– Keith Taylor

RAMBLES AROUND MANCHESTER
– Mike Cresswell

WESTERN LAKELAND RAMBLES
– Gordon Brown

WELSH WALKS:
Dolgellau and the Cambrian Coast
– Laurence Main and Morag Perrott

WELSH WALKS:
Aberystwyth and District
– Laurence Main and Morag Perrott

– all of these books are currently £6.95 each.